BRAVO!

BRAVO!

The inside story
of the Atlanta Braves'
1995 World Series Championship

BY I.J. ROSENBERG
AND THE PHOTOGRAPHY STAFF
OF THE ATLANTA JOURNAL-CONSTITUTION

ACKNOWLEDGMENTS

In baseball lingo, I'm hitting .600 — three books in five seasons on the Braves beat. (There were two manuscripts that went unpublished, thanks to the Phillies in 1993 and the strike in 1994.)

That's a pretty good batting average. But I couldn't have done it without a lot of help.

I'm grateful to Robert Mashburn, who designed the first two books and added the task of editing this one.

I'm grateful to the photography staff of the Atlanta Journal-Constitution, especially Calvin Cruce, who went through hundreds of rolls of film to choose the pictures you see in this book.

I'm grateful for the support I've received from the management teams at Cox Enterprises and the Atlanta Journal-Constitution, from newspaper division president Jay Smith (a huge baseball fan), and from former publisher Dennis Berry, editor Ron Martin and managing editor John Walter.

I'd also like to thank:

Sports editor Don Boykin, whose door is always open, and assistant Dinn Mann, the department's new star, who gave me many new ideas.

Tim Tucker and Mark Bradley, who love the game as much as I do, and Jack Wilkinson and the other co-workers with whom I spent countless hours at the ballpark.

Furman Bisher, the greatest sportswriter I've read, who helped bring the Braves to Atlanta.

The friends at Longstreet Press and publisher Chuck Perry.

And finally, the Braves, for some of the most memorable times of my life, and for a title I never thought my hometown would get.

I.J. ROSENBERG

DEDICATION

To Beth Ann, Ashley, Lindsey and Chase, the greatest team in the world.

FOREWORD

In the spring there was little indication that such joy was ahead. The mood was sullen. Major leaguers stayed home while applicants for their jobs took the field in Florida and Arizona. When an uncertain peace did settle over the game, the Braves got away to a plodding start. At one time they were five games behind Philadelphia. Accordingly, the fans were slow to come back.

In time, the nightmare would turn into a dream. Those sullen times dissolved into a distant blur. Could this be real? Were we hallucinating, or was this parade down Peachtree actually in celebration of a World Series that didn't get away?

They had conquered all, swept the season championship by 21 games, reeled through Colorado and Cincinnati like a destructive storm, then choked down the Indians with pitching. There had

been some presumptuous speculation in the spring, when Marquis Grissom was brought home, that this might be one of those teams to be compared with the finest in major league history, usually measured by the 1927 Yankees or the 1930 Athletics. Whatever their caliber, these Braves brought the city its finest moment in professional history, dotted with occasional minor league successes of the old Atlanta Crackers. So brilliant was Tom Glavine in the game that cinched it that Greg Maddux's brilliance in Game 1 was lost in the afterglow. David Justice supplied the only run needed when he sent a shot over the rightfield fence that sealed his peace with the fans whose feathers he had ruffled.

Now, they paraded. They had achieved the crest. They were the champions of all they surveyed and Atlanta ascended along with them. This was a moment to be framed forever in one's mental scrapbook. As slow as fans had been to take them back to the bosom, when they made the turn into September and the race became a jaunt, the romance was renewed. The third time had been the charm. Take another flight back into history and find that the Yankees lost their first two World Series, then set off on the most dominating championship run known to man. Not to suggest another dynasty here, but of such are dynasties born. Here it is chronicled by the man who has seen it from the first victory to the hoisting of the flag, I.J. Rosenberg. It seems a bit sad that Chuck Tanner couldn't have been somewhere on the scene, for it was he, when made manager of the Braves, who foresaw all this. "There'll be a big parade down Peachtree Street with confetti for the championship Braves," Tanner said in that ebullient moment. But that's what memories are for.

So now they cheer their Braves, World Champions of baseball. Roll that around in your mind for a moment. What an easy and delectable phrase. They stand proud and the city stands proud alongside, happy and aglow. You can say you were there when it happened, and now read of it as it takes its proper place in the diary of the place that began life as Marthasville.

FURMAN BISHER

CHAPTER 1

JOURNEY'S END

THE SCOREBOARD CLOCK, SHINING BRIGHTLY ABOVE THE left-field wall at Atlanta-Fulton County Stadium, read 10:26 p.m.

The crowd was on its feet, screaming, chopping, clapping, the noise climbing to a maddening level. All eyes were on Braves reliever Mark Wohlers, standing straight and tall on the mound, his cap pulled down low on his forehead, facing the plate straight on, hands poised in front of his body, the ball hidden inside his glove.

Catcher Javier Lopez flashed the sign, flicking down the index and middle fingers on his right hand, signaling for a split-finger fastball.

The batter, Carlos Baerga, dug in, his feet planted squarely, his bat steady, his eyes intently on the pitcher.

Wohlers lifted his big left leg high into the air, rocked back and flung his right arm forward, sending the ball speeding and spinning toward the plate.

The batter swung, and the ball soared toward left center field as the clock clicked to 10:27. Center fielder Marquis Grissom, off at the crack of the bat, sped across the green outfield grass.

In the press box, my fingers poised over the computer, my mind flashed back to a lifetime of Braves memories,

Mark Wohlers, Javier Lopez and Chipper Jones converged on the mound and were quickly buried by onrushing teammates.

Opposite page: MARLENE KARAS

Previous page: RENEE HANNANS

David Justice provided the only run the Braves would need to win the championship, blasting a solo home run in the sixth inning.

THE 1995 ATLANTA BRAVES

from Henry Aaron to Dale Murphy, from Luman Harris to Bobby Cox, a lifetime of disappointment.

Then Grissom reached for the sky and snatched the ball out of the night air.

I began typing:

It ended Saturday at 10:27 p.m. It ended all the heartbreak, the misery, the years of suffering this city has endured with its professional sports teams.

I looked over the press box overhang and saw my father, just a few rows below, jumping and hugging and grabbing everyone around. A native Atlantan, a longtime season ticket holder, he had waited so long for this moment.

Taste it, Atlanta. Feel it. Breathe it. You have a world champion.

Wohlers raised both arms and jumped into the air, again and again. The other players rushed the mound, Lopez leading the charge and launching himself into Wohlers' arms. Chipper Jones raced in from third base, and soon the pitcher and catcher were buried under a sea of white uniforms. The sounds of Queen's "We Are The Champions" engulfed the stadium. In

BRAVO!

Tom Glavine limited the Indians to one hit in eight innings before Mark Wohlers came on to close it out in the ninth.

MARLENE KARAS

7

the stands and on the field, the cheering and screaming and hugging went on and on. Bobby Cox raised his fists in the air. Ted Turner was dancing. Some people were crying.

In a game where Tom Glavine pitched his heart out and David Justice won back the fans' hearts, the Braves turned a town giddy and ended the World Series with a 1-0 win over the Cleveland Indians before 51,875 screaming, dancing and chopping fans at Atlanta-Fulton County Stadium. And they may still be dancing down Peachtree Street this morning.

Later, the players ran back onto the field after their lockerroom celebration, many of them joined by their families. They wore world championship T-shirts, world championship hats. Champagne spewed everywhere. Turner paraded in front of the dugout with the World Series trophy, then stopped to take pictures with the grounds crew. Stan Kasten hugged John Schuerholz's wife. Pitching coach Leo Mazzone hoisted two champagne bottles, one in each hand. Cox grinned from ear to ear.

Glavine, the Series MVP, talked to the media. He had been masterful, pitching eight innings and allowing just one base hit, a soft bloop single into left field by Tony Peña in the sixth inning.

"I wanted to win this as badly as anything I wanted to win in my life," said Glavine, who had endured much criticism for his role as a player representative during the strike. "None of us wanted to go through another winter with another close defeat hanging over our heads."

Justice, whose sixth-inning homer scored the only run, signed autographs. Just hours before, he had been booed lustily as fans responded to his comments in the paper the morning of the game. "Where's the parade if we lose?" he had asked. "If we don't win, they'll probably run us out of town."

"I did it because I wanted our fans to prove us wrong," he said after the game. "To come out and prove Dave Justice wrong. And they did. They were awesome out there."

Wohlers was asked about the final out.

"As soon as I heard the fans cheering, I blacked out," he said. "I didn't know what the hell to do. Then I saw Javy running at me and I knew I'd better stop or he'd blow me away."

Cox never stopped smiling. He kept looking at the scoreboard, which still burned with the final score: Braves 1, Indians 0.

In the stands, long after the game, a little boy and his father remained in their seats, doing the chop.

World champions. Taste it. Feel it. Breathe it.

Atlanta had its first major championship. The journey that began in 1991 had come to a triumphant end on this chilly October night.

MARLENE KARAS

BRAVO!

CHAPTER 2

SPRING, SPRING

I T WAS A LONG, MISERABLE WINTER — AND THE WEATHER
wasn't very good, either. "Collective bargaining"
became the nastiest term in baseball. From
Washington to New York to Chicago, I followed the owners and players as they tried to reach a new economic
agreement. It became a war of words, and the distrust
grew with each failed negotiation. The players hated the
owners. The owners hated the players. Their eternal
haggling shut down a $2 billion industry in which every-
one was making plenty of money.

The strike was in its seventh month when the owners
decided to start spring training without the major leaguers. As I stepped out of the West Palm Beach airport
on Feb. 17, I wasn't looking forward to the weeks ahead.

Spring training is usually a great time of year. The
Florida sun always feels good after several months in
the cold. The players, fans and media seem to enjoy the
relaxed atmosphere, and they take advantage of the
chance to grab some rays and play some golf.

But this year the regulars were at home and a camp
full of replacement players — or scabs, as the major leaguers called them — were waiting.

At Municipal Stadium, the only person in the cubby-

*Many fans,
alienated by the
strike, welcomed
the replacement
players with
open arms.*

hole that serves as the media room was Braves public relations director Jim Schultz, who didn't look too thrilled himself. Jim is one of the nicest people in the game, but he didn't look forward to this new brand of baseball.

The major-league clubhouse was empty. There was nothing hanging in the lockers. Not even the nameplates had been put up. Bobby Cox said the replacement players would dress in the minor league clubhouse, which was more like a barn with hundreds of stalls. After a few days, it smelled awful in there.

That's how the championship season started, with Tom Glavine and Greg Maddux and Steve Avery at home playing golf; with Charlie O'Brien tend-

FRANK NIEMEIR

More than 100 players were in camp with the Braves, some of them hoping to be replacements ... and some avoiding that label at all costs.

ing cows on his ranch in Oklahoma; with David Justice on the set of his wife's movie. They were supposed to be stretching in the Florida sun, working into shape for another season. But there was no Mark Lemke, no Fred McGriff, no Rafael Belliard.

Instead, there were so many replacement players that it was impossible to remember names. The replacements were mixed in with the minor leaguers, which meant going to every player in camp to ask if they would be a replacement.

These players had been threatened by the union. Anyone who crossed the line would be ostracized by the major leaguers. But the Braves and other teams were offering $115,000 a year to those who made the team. That was

The replacement players were lured by the chance to earn $115,000 a season … and the chance to pursue a dream that many of them had lost.

a lot of money for these players; many of them had spent years bouncing around the minor leagues, making as little as $1,000 a month. The lure of the big leagues brought out all kinds. At the Mets camp in Port St. Lucie, there was a fat refrigerator salesman who could actually throw a pretty good fastball. He made headlines in the New York tabloids.

One of the first players I met in Braves camp was Rod Nichols, a journeyman pitcher with an 11-26 career record. Before I could ask, Nichols declared: "I'm not a scab and I would appreciate it if you would put that in the paper. I don't want to be associated with those guys. I don't think they should even be in here with us." Give me a break. Did he think they had some kind of disease?

But statements like that came out of every camp. At the Marlins camp up the road in Melbourne, reliever Richie Lewis, who was trying to earn his way back to the majors, said, "I think (the clubs) should put red stickers on the replacement players' heads."

The Braves coaches went about the business of trying to put together a team, deciding who would play in exhibition games and who wouldn't. Cox really didn't do much, riding in his golf cart from one field to another and playing golf just about every day.

FRANK NIEMEIR

The Braves staffer most bothered was pitching coach Leo Mazzone. The Fab Five had spoiled him, and now he was working with pitchers who would never be in camp if not for the strike. Day after day, I would walk into the coaches' room and ask Leo how his pitchers were doing.

"Don't want to talk about it," he would grumble. The other coaches would laugh. But it was hard on everyone, because they all knew this eventually would not matter.

When the spring training games started, I called a few of the major leaguers to see what they were doing.

Jeff Blauser, who was a free agent, was in Atlanta. "I'm retired," he said.

Maddux was at his home in Las Vegas. "I'm doing what I usually do before spring training, playing golf," he said. "I'm not getting on a mound."

Mark Wohlers had just left his job at a body shop. "I've been throwing on my own," he said.

John Smoltz was home in Atlanta. "I get a feeling, whether I'm on the golf

Fans turned out for replacement baseball, but they made their feelings about the strike known.

THE 1995 ATLANTA BRAVES

Leo Mazzone, accustomed to the Braves' all-star staff, struggled to find decent pitchers among the less-talented replacements.

course, baby-sitting or whatever, I'm not doing what I'm supposed to be doing," he said. "My body and mind ache for baseball."

The games with the replacement players were not good baseball. They weren't laughable, but they weren't smooth. None of the hitters had much power. But the games went on. The fans cheered the replacement players and seemed to respect them for what they were doing. Everything was fairly quiet and uneventful.

But on March 25, a bombshell.

Early in the day, the Braves lost their fourth straight. My wife, father and father-in-law were in town. When we came back from dinner, I was checking the paper's wire services for baseball news with the television on in the background. I heard the show being interrupted.

"Just in, a Braves replacement player has been murdered. We'll be back at 11 with details."

FRANK NIEMEIR

Pat Corrales and the other coaches worked hard with the replacements, all the time not knowing if they would ever play.

PALM BEACH POST

Pitcher Dave Shotkoski (above, far right) was killed near the Braves' hotel, leaving behind his wife Felicia and baby daughter Alexis (right).

ASSOCIATED PRESS

BRAVO!

My stomach dropped. I called the office and told them something was going on. A friend at the Palm Beach Post verified the story. The player was pitcher Dave Shotkoski, a 30-year-old righthander who had not played professionally since reaching the Class AA level in 1991. He was working for Coca-Cola in suburban Chicago, and the company had given him permission to chase his dream. He had the first locker to the right when you walked in the clubhouse. He had a wife and an infant daughter.

I wrote a late story, but the facts were still sketchy. The next day at camp, almost everyone seemed in shock. Several players were crying. The game was called off, and most of the players left camp early.

The crime scene was on the edge of the worst part of town, near the Braves' minor league hotel. Shotkoski had been out for a walk when someone on a bike stopped and tried to rob him. There was a confrontation and Shotkoski was shot. There was a path of blood where he had tried to drag himself to the street. He died as his head hit the pavement.

Everyone in camp seemed stunned and saddened. But one player was spurred to action.

Terry Blocker, a former Brave who was trying to earn a job as a replacement player, had become friends with Shotkoski. They first noticed each other when Blocker hit a line drive back through the pitcher's legs in an intersquad game. They talked in the lockerroom the next day, and the friendship grew. Blocker noticed the picture of Shotkoski's eight-month-old daughter hanging in his locker. They spoke of family and, later, of religion. Their last conversation ended when both had to leave to wire home their paychecks.

When Blocker heard the news, he was devastated. He cried as he thought of Shotkoski's wife, Felicia, and little girl Alexis. And he knew he had to do something. He had to help find the killer. He hit the streets around the drug-infested area where Shotkoski was killed. "I knew it was a bad place, but I can't be scared of my own people," said Blocker.

His courage and determination paid off. He uncovered information that helped lead police to an arrest. The man, a habitual criminal, was charged with the murder.

"When I last played here in 1989, I had met a guy who was a little down on his luck and needed some money," Blocker said. "I gave him some. He found out this spring that I was back with the team and called me up. I called him right after Dave was shot and we went into the neighborhood.

CHARLOTTE B. TEAGLE

Terry Blocker (with wife LaFrancine, son T.J. and daughter LaTerrica) was devastated by Dave Shotkoski's murder.

DAVID TULIS

Tom Glavine, an outspoken player representative during the strike, was still a hit with some fans.

"I was down there Friday night and some parts of Saturday and Sunday. At first people wouldn't talk. But he (the alleged killer) bragged to some people about it and some people told me. I found out where he had been hanging out. Police told me it was a crack house about six months ago. I told the police Saturday, and sure enough he came back there the next day."

The man was arrested on Sunday. On Monday, Blocker was cut.

A few days later, it was like Shotkoski had never been there. The Braves cut to a 25-man roster, broke camp and headed to Atlanta for three exhibitions. Only two would be played.

On March 31, a New York judge ruled that the owners had illegally implemented an economic system. The players called off their strike when the owners agreed to return to business under the old system, the one that led to the strike in the first place. There was no agreement on a new deal. All the meetings, all the talk, had solved nothing.

The Braves called off the final game and sent the replacements on their way with an extra $5,000 for their trouble.

"We sort of knew this was coming," said replacement player Mike Bell. "But it still hurts."

The major leaguers headed to Florida. Another spring training, another three weeks in West Palm Beach. Everything had to be done quickly. The

DAVID TULIS

The Braves regulars arrived in West Palm Beach with three weeks to prepare for the season — half the normal time.

DAVID TULIS

David Justice and the other Braves welcomed the arrival of Marquis Grissom, a native of Atlanta who was obtained in a trade with the Expos.

season was less than three weeks away, leaving major leaguers with half the time they normally have to get ready.

The first day the players hit camp, Glavine, who had been criticized for his role as a player representative in the strike, spent extra time signing autographs. He had been a target on radio talk shows in Atlanta all winter. He was hurt, but he was also smart — he was trying to win back the fans.

"There are going to be a fair number of people who are going to be resentful toward us," he said. "We're going to make a concerted effort to be accommodating to fans and try to win back those people who have sworn off the game."

It sounded nice. But there weren't enough players with that attitude. Neither side did a lot to get the fans back, and they would pay for it.

The Braves' front office was scrambling. Negotiations with Blauser were going nowhere. Then general manager John Schuerholz pulled off a great deal, getting Marquis Grissom from the Expos to bat leadoff and play center field. It was a quick deal, done in two days. Expos general manager Kevin Malone was holding a fire sale — he also traded away John Wetteland and Ken Hill that week, and did not sign Larry Walker — because the team's owners told him to cut his payroll dramatically.

The Braves gave up a lot to get Grissom, sending Roberto Kelly, Tony Tarasco and a pitching prospect to Montreal. But Schuerholz loved the deal. He felt Grissom was the missing piece of the puzzle.

"It looks like we gave up an awful lot," he said, "but look at the deal, look at the type of player we're getting."

It was a steal. Kelly wasn't a true leadoff hitter and there was no room in the Atlanta outfield for Tarasco. Grissom was one of the most exciting players in baseball, and he's from Atlanta.

After that deal, it was a pretty uneventful spring. The Braves eventually worked out a deal for Blauser when his agent, Scott Boras, convinced the Braves that the Texas Rangers were bidding for the shortstop's services. Blauser got $10 million for three years, a deal that would turn out to be the Braves' worst move of the season.

When the team broke camp and headed to Atlanta, they were greeted by a big yawn. An exhibition game against the Yankees drew just 8,000. The two spring trainings were over, but baseball wasn't the same. The players were back, but the fans were not.

The Braves faced the fans after a preseason workout, answering questions about the strike.

FRANK NIEMEIR

BRAVO!

CHAPTER 3

REGULAR SEASON RUNAWAY

IT WAS ABOUT THE MIDDLE OF JULY WHEN THE BRAVES began to realize that this year was different. The Dodgers, Giants and Reds, great antagonists of past pennant races, had been banished to other divisions. The Phillies, newly cast in the villain's role, were fading faster than an old newspaper.

The heat of summer was still with us, and the Braves were running away with the National League East. There would be no need for stretch-run heroics.

"It was different, not having that intense September that we're used to," said pitcher John Smoltz. "But I think it was good, because it gave everyone a chance to work on stuff without worrying about the division. The pitchers were able to stay a lot stronger, and it paid off in October."

The regular season may have lacked drama, but it was not without significant moments.

Wednesday, April 26: The strike was over. The regulars were back. The season had been cut to 144 games, and the Giants were in town for the opener.

On a beautiful, sunny afternoon, 24,091 fans turned out to see the Braves roll to a 12-5 win. It was the only time all season the team announced the number of fans

Even the best seats often went unused early in the season. There were thousands of no-shows at most games.

DAVID TULIS

Bravo!

Fans weren't shy about displaying their opinions of baseball's labor problems, both inside the stadium and out.

DAVID TULIS

ANDY SHARP

in the ballpark. From then on, they announced the number of tickets sold, leaving thousands of no-shows unaccounted for each game.

Monday, May 8: The Braves were struggling. They had lost three straight to the Phillies over the weekend, then awoke to learn their manager had been arrested overnight for allegedly assaulting his wife, Pam. It was a very strange day in the clubhouse. The players were shocked, but stood behind their manager. "Life brings bumps along the way," said reliever Steve Bedrosian. "It's important that he knows he's our leader and we support him and Pam." That night, Cox was back in the dugout, and the Braves were beaten by the Phillies again, 3-2. It was the first time they had been swept in a four-game series since 1990.

Sunday, May 14: Owner Ted Turner attended his first game of the season. He didn't seem worried by the small crowds or the Braves' 8-9 record. "I hope someday the fans will be back, and I hope someday we'll be back in first place," he said. For the second time in three days, the Reds' Ron Gant beat his former teammates with a game-winning home run. "I can't understand why someone hasn't stepped up and done more," Cox said. "We've got to get it straight and that's my job."

Monday, June 5: Something was still wrong. The Braves had lost five straight and the talk shows were lighting up. Tom Glavine called the first (and only) team meeting of the season. "We know we are not playing well," Glavine said. "But I don't think that you can interpret that as complacency. The attitude around here right now is a little more down than usual. But we're not going to panic." Cox shook up the lineup that night, putting rookie Brad Kowitz in the leadoff spot and moving Marquis Grissom to second in the order. The Braves responded by beating the Cubs 7-5, with Mark Wohlers collecting the club's first save since May 18. The next night, Ryan Klesko hit two home runs, including a grand slam, and the Braves won 17-3.

Monday, June 12: As the Braves' Delta charter taxied to the runway at Hartsfield, the cabin suddenly filled with smoke. Everyone had to slide down the emergency chutes. The evacuation of the 52 players, coaches and support personnel took only one minute. The problem was caused by hydraulic fluid from mechanisms at the tail of the plane dripping onto a hot engine. The fluid vaporized and the air conditioning unit sucked it into the cabin.

"We started to see smoke coming from under our feet," said rookie Mike Mordecai. "Ryan thought somebody was playing a joke on us, like in the minor leagues when they set your shoelaces on fire."

Jeff Blauser took it as a sign. "The last time we saw smoke (in 1993, when the stadium press box caught fire before Fred McGriff's first game as a Brave), we went on a pretty good run," he said. He was right. The Braves moved to another plane, flew to Montreal and started a seven-game winning streak.

THE 1995 ATLANTA BRAVES

ERIK S. LESSER

Ninth-inning wins: Dwight Smith's grand slam beat the Marlins, and David Justice's two-run blast beat the Expos.

Sunday, July 2: Before the major league's biggest crowd of the season to date (59,203 at Veterans Stadium), the Braves beat Philadelphia for the third time in four games and cut the Phillies' lead from three games to one.

Wednesday, July 5: The Braves got their first look at Dodgers rookie sensation Hideo Nomo, a pitcher from the Japanese Leagues who had become a national celebrity back home. Scattered throughout the Atlanta-Fulton County Stadium crowd that night were little groups of Japanese fans, including one woman who came all the way from Japan for the game. "I called her and said I got tickets, so why don't you come?" explained Masami Suzuki, a student at Georgia State. "So I came," said Junko Inose, a Fuji Bank employee in Tokyo.

Nomo looked great against Braves, but Smoltz was just as good. The Braves' only run against Nomo came on a wild pitch, and both starters departed with the scored tied 1-1. Chipper Jones hit a three-run homer in the bottom of the ninth to win it, putting the Braves alone in first.

Sunday, July 9: The Braves blew into the All-Star break on a nine-game

Opposite page: DAVID TULIS

BRAVO!

JONATHAN NEWTON

BRAVO!

John Smoltz and Dodgers sensation Hideo Nomo battled to a standoff for eight innings, but the Braves won in the ninth on a home run by Chipper Jones.

Rookie Chipper Jones won games with his bat and his glove, despite on-the-job training at third base.

FRANK NIEMEIR

BRAVO!

winning streak, thanks to McGriff's three-run homer in the ninth that beat the Giants. Atlanta led the East by four games, after trailing by five just 15 days earlier.

Saturday, July 15: Blauser and Dwight Smith hit seventh-inning homers to beat the Padres 7-6. It was the Braves' 12th win in their last 13 games, and they led the Phillies by six games. "This is why I came here, because of games like this," said catcher Charlie O'Brien. "Every night we have a chance."

The labor dispute rose to the surface while the team was in San Diego. Padres general manager Randy Smith considered calling up a former replacement player from the minors, but changed his mind when the players made it clear they did not want him on the squad. "This was cut-and-dried, black-and-white," said the Padres' Bip Roberts. "Right now, the way the chemistry is in this clubhouse, we don't want any distractions." What chemistry? The Padres had just lost nine of 11 games.

Mark Wohlers took over the closer's job in early June and converted his first 19 save opportunities.

Leo Mazzone kept his pitching staff healthy again. The rotation missed only one start all season.

Would John Schuerholz have asked Braves players before bringing up a replacement player? He wouldn't say. "I don't think anybody thinks John Schuerholz has to do it," Glavine said. "But what Randy Smith did was a classy thing. It shows he has respect for his players."

(Later in the year, Schuerholz considered bringing up Dale Polley, a former replacement player who was at Class AAA Richmond. But he never made the move.)

Friday, July 21: The Braves gave Cox a two-year extension. "I couldn't ask for a better place to manage. I'll be here to the year 2000," said Cox, who was making $600,000 a season and received a small raise. "The raise is nothing that would knock your eyes out, but I'm not hard to please." Some wondered if Cox would be back after the incident with his wife. "We recognize that we have to deal with human issues," said Schuerholz. "I think he has dealt with them very well."

The 1995 Atlanta Braves

41

Reserve infielder Mike Mordecai had
several key hits during the season, including
a three-run homer against San Francisco.

JONATHAN NEWTON

Friday, Aug. 11: Steve Bedrosian, given the option of retiring or being released, chose the former. He was very upset, though, and didn't hang around to tell his teammates goodbye. Later that day, the Braves acquired Luis Polonia from the Yankees, sending minor league outfielder Troy Hughes to New York. Meanwhile, the Braves were rolling along with a 62-35 record and a 13 1/2 game lead.

Tuesday, Aug. 22: The Astros, trailing by two runs in the seventh, had the bases loaded with two out. Tony Eusebio ripped a ball down the third-base line that looked like a bases-clearing double. But Jones dived to his right, snared the ball, jumped up and threw out Eusebio by a step. It was the Braves' defensive play of the season. "I don't really know how I made the play. It was just a reflex," Jones said.

Friday, Aug. 25: The Braves traded disgruntled third baseman Jose Oliva to the Cardinals and acquired Mike Devereaux from the White Sox. Devereaux gave the Braves a badly needed right-handed bat off the bench.

Before the game that day at Wrigley Field, singer Elton John made an appearance around the Braves' batting cage. John, a part-time Atlanta resident and long-time Braves fan, posed for photos with players, gave autographs and talked a terrific game of baseball.

Even Cox was impressed. The manager started cracking up when John second-guessed his removal of Mark Lemke from the No. 2 spot in the batting order. "He was batting OK at No. 2," John argued.

Cox said the Braves had gotten feedback from John before. "It's funny," he said. "Whenever we do something good or have a streak, we receive a telegram from Elton. But there is no return address to write him back. I can thank him now."

This was John's first visit to a major league ballgame. He was in town for two nights of performances at the nearby United Center. The pregame meeting was arranged by Braves traveling secretary Bill Acree, who escorted John around the field and received tickets to Friday night's show.

"I had never gone to a game because I didn't want to ever cause a commotion," John said. "But I thought this would be perfect with the Braves playing, and (Wrigley Field) is just a great place. I have always been a big Braves fan, even in the dog days, and I watch them on television all the time. I used to watch (Phil) Niekro and (Dale) Murphy. And I really like baseball; there is no sport that is more romantic."

Thursday, Aug. 31: The Braves made their final move of the season, getting Alejandro Peña from the Marlins. Going into the final month, the club was relaxed and, with a 14-game lead, Cox was able to make sure his regulars were well rested.

Wednesday, Sept. 13: The Braves popped the cork at 35,000 feet on

Marquis Grissom became the first Atlanta native to start for the Braves.

the Delta charter after clinching their fourth straight division championship. They had clinched a tie that afternoon with a win over the Rockies, and the title became official a few hours later when the Phillies lost to the Expos.

Sunday, Sept. 17: The Braves wrapped up a three-game sweep of the Reds. The series had been billed a preview of the League Championship Series, and that turned out to be exactly right. Greg Maddux, Glavine and Smoltz were dominating — limiting the Reds to a .216 average — just as they were in the NLCS. Reds manager Davey Johnson was glad to see the Braves leave town, saying, "I'll drive the bus if they need me to."

Wednesday, Sept. 27: Maddux got his 19th win of the season and 150th of his career, beating the Phillies 6-0. The rest of the Braves were rolling, too. The Rockies awaited in the first round of the expanded playoffs.

Fred McGriff failed to hit 30 home runs for the first time in eight seasons, but he still had plenty of big hits, including a game-winner against the Giants.

Shortstop Jeff Blauser and starter Steve Avery both struggled in '95, Blauser hitting .211 and Avery posting a 7-13 record.

RICH ADDICKS

JONATHAN NEWTON

JONATHAN NEWTON

BRAVO!

CHAPTER 4

GREG MADDUX, REGULAR GUY

'LL NEVER FORGET MY FIRST FACE-TO-FACE ENCOUNTER with Greg Maddux. It was in February 1993, as Greg reported to West Palm Beach for his first spring training with the Braves.

He walked into the clubhouse wearing an old pair of shorts, a wrinkled shirt and no socks. He was skinny, he had a small pot belly, and there was a pinch of snuff in his top lip. My first thought was, how could this be the next great pitcher in baseball? He didn't look like a $28 million man to me.

Greg's appearance has never really changed. But his astonishing performance since joining the Braves leaves no question that he's one of the most amazing athletes in sports. He now has four straight Cy Young awards, and he just keeps getting better. Over the past two seasons, he's 35-8 with a 1.60 ERA.

The best thing about Greg, though, is his personality. He's friendly, honest and easy-going. How can you not like a guy who calls everybody dude?

Hey, dude. What's up, dude? It's cool, dude. See ya, dude.

Last winter, I went to Las Vegas to do a story on him and discovered he's the same at home as he is at the ballpark.

The best thing about Greg Maddux is his personality. He's friendly, honest and easy-going.

Greg Maddux's
Cy Young Awards
hang at the top of
the stairs of his
offseason home
in Las Vegas.

His neighborhood, called Spanish Trails, is made up of two-story Spanish Tudor homes that all look alike and are only a few feet apart. It's a nice area, but not extravagant. Quiet. Subtle. A lot like Greg.

"We're not out to impress anybody," says his wife, Kathy. "We're not out to say, 'Oh, we've got this much money, we have to make sure everybody knows about it.' I know a lot of people say that. But I think it's one thing to say it and one thing to live it."

Inside the house, you'd never know a great baseball player lives there — except for the Cy Young plaques at the top of the stairs. In the family room, there's a huge television hooked up to a Nintendo (a habit picked up when he was in the minors). Everything is neat, but not because of Greg. Kathy has to pick up after him.

On a typical off-season day, Greg plays golf in the morning and comes home in the afternoon to take care of his baby daughter Amanda. Greg is very good with Amanda; they even take naps together.

When Greg came home from the golf course the day I was there, Kathy had to talk him into taking a shower. (This is nothing new. During spring training, his teammates are always giving him a hard time about throwing on his clothes after a workout and heading straight to the golf course.)

Greg never combs his hair, either. "He doesn't like how his hair looks when he combs it," Kathy says. "When we go out to dinner and a hockey game, he wears a hat. When we visit friends, he wears a hat. But that's all right. He's not trying to impress anyone that he's Mr. Smooth."

His mother, Linda, was visiting, and she watched Amanda while Kathy went to Wendy's to get lunch for everyone. After wolfing down a couple of burgers and some fries, Greg was ready to meet the local media. When reporters and cameramen from two television stations came over, Mrs. Maddux begged her son to put on some shoes. He wouldn't, so Mrs. Maddux asked the cameramen not to show his bare feet. They complied.

The next day, Greg invited me to play golf at the Tournament Players Club, where a PGA Tour event had concluded the day before. Maddux loves the course; he plays there at least four times a week during the winter. His brother Mike, who at the time was pitching for the Mets, played with us. Mike's a better golfer. He has a better swing.

But Greg is the same on the golf course as he is on the mound — tough. Last spring, he played in a charity tournament where on one hole, everyone had to hit their tee shot with the opposite hand. Maddux normally swings right-handed, so he had to hit his tee shot left-handed. Everyone dribbled their first shot off the tee, including Maddux. His ball sat 315 yards from the green. But he pulled out a driver, drew it back (swinging right-handed now) and whacked the ball just off the front of the green. Then he chipped in for a birdie, the only one on the hole that day. That's tough.

That day we played in Las Vegas, Maddux shot a 78. A few weeks later,

Greg Maddux plays golf almost every day during the offseason. His favorite course is the Tournament Players Club in Las Vegas.

*Greg Maddux
rarely takes full
credit for victories,
instead praising
the defense, the
hitters or the
bullpen.*

THE 1995 ATLANTA BRAVES

when a reporter from Sports Illustrated came out to do a story, he shot a 70 — and that's the round the whole sports world read about. That's tough.

Greg's family moved to Las Vegas when he was in high school, and he loves the area. He can live peacefully there without fans and the media always bugging him. The bright lights are limited to The Strip.

"I think that is why we like Vegas so much," Kathy says. "A lot of the players in Atlanta, anytime they go anywhere, either people are on them about the strike or asking them about the strike. We can go out here and nobody really recognizes him. And if they do, they are not so obsessed with baseball that they ask him a million questions."

Maddux's dad deals blackjack at one of the local casinos, and Greg has been known to visit The Strip. One night when the family went to dinner, the bill came to $150. At the end of the meal, Greg went over to a blackjack table, put $150 on one hand and drew a winner. He's got a reputation for being a terrific poker player. He notices things — such as another player moving his chips around whenever he has a good hand — that help him win.

Greg is no dummy on the mound, either. In a game early this season against the Mets, he had worked the count to 1-and-2 against Ryan Thompson when the game was halted by rain. The tarp was pulled out and Maddux went into the clubhouse. About 30 minutes later, the rain stopped and Maddux returned to the dugout. He noticed Thompson taking practice swings and saw that he was swinging as if he were expecting an inside pitch. So when the game resumed, Maddux threw a slider away and got a strikeout.

Maddux has been known to intentionally throw a ball on a 2-and-2 pitch because he knows he can come back and get the hitter out on a 3-and-2 changeup. The other Braves pitchers will sometimes bet on whether he'll do it. Maddux's strategy works because a major-league hitter just can't believe a pitcher would throw a changeup on a full count.

The best way to describe how Maddux's pitches always seem to miss the hitter's bat is to borrow a few lines from a Sports Illustrated story by Tom Verducci:

"Imagine an inclined trough carrying water to home plate. Then imagine a post in front of the center of the plate. The rushing water will flow away from the post and toward the outsides of the plate. That's exactly the flow of Maddux's pitches. Everything moves away from the center of the plate. The nightmare for a hitter is guessing which of Maddux's five pitches is coming and which direction it's flowing. Some hitters try to reduce the permutations by looking for the ball in a certain area, but Maddux defeats that strategy by noticing subtleties that give away whether those hitters are looking for a ball in or a ball away."

Maddux spends some time before each start studying the lineup card, but

Greg Maddux keeps his information on opposing hitters in his head, and he never forgets.

Kathy Maddux (above right, with Carri Glavine) says she and Greg enjoy relative obscurity in Las Vegas.

he keeps his information on opposing hitters in his head. He never forgets. If he makes a hitter look bad on a pitch, he remembers it.

"You save it for when you need it again," he says. "It might be late in the game with runners on base. It might not be until the next time you face that team. It might not be for two years."

Even the best hitters are awed by him. Six-time batting champion Tony Gwynn says, "He's like a meticulous surgeon out there. Most guys are afraid to pitch inside because if you make a mistake there, you're going to get hurt. But he puts the ball where he wants to. And that cutter (cut fastball) can be a nightmare. You see a pitch inside and you wonder, 'Is it the fastball or the cutter?' That's where he's got you."

With each start this season, Maddux seemed to get stronger. And afterward, he would always say it was because of his defense or the bullpen or the runs his team scored. He never takes full credit.

He keeps the same low profile off the field. He does no commercials, and he often goes unnoticed in public.

"I'll be out with him," says teammate John Smoltz, "and people will say, 'Hey, there's John Smoltz,' and nothing else. I've seen it happen at home, in Atlanta. He can walk right through a crowd of people."

Looking back on these last three seasons with Maddux, it's easy to wish all athletes were like him. I've never seen him turn down an autograph. He's always willing to talk to the media after the game, and he never has anything unpleasant to say about anyone.

Greg Maddux won his fourth straight Cy Young Award and also received some MVP votes.

DAVID TULIS

CHAPTER 5

YOUTH IS SERVED

HIS NAME IS LARRY WAYNE JONES. NOT MANY PEOPLE know that, except his teammates, and they tease him about it unmercifully.

Not since David Justice in 1990 has a rookie had such an impact on the Braves. Beyond Greg Maddux, he may have been the club's MVP. When the Braves needed a big hit, he delivered. When they needed a big defensive play, he was in the air — or on the ground — making it happen.

But just where did Chipper Jones get that nickname?

"Just a chip off the ol' block," he says.

Jones, 23, was the Braves' most consistent offensive player this season, throughout the regular season and into the playoffs. And his defense at third base, a position he'd never played before this season, was steady — and at times spectacular.

"What an incredible season he had," said manager Bobby Cox. "Everything we asked him to do, he did and more. How many players can come into the league and step right into the shoes of a guy like Terry Pendleton?"

Jones is one of four young players who give this franchise a bright outlook on the future. The others:

Reliever Mark Wohlers, who has been around since

Chipper Jones played solid defense at third base, a position he had never played before this season.

Opposite page: JONATHAN NEWTON

1991 but is only 25. He blossomed into the dominating closer the Braves have been seeking for years.

Left fielder Ryan Klesko, who averaged a home run every 14.3 at-bats during the regular season, then homered on three consecutive nights in the World Series.

Catcher Javier Lopez, who hit .315 during the season and blasted clutch homers in the NLCS and World Series.

Jones is the type player who could become Atlanta's next Dale Murphy — someone who thrills with his bat, glove ... and personality. Jones is swarmed by autograph seekers wherever

TAIMY ALVAREZ

he goes. And when the team needed a spark in late May, it was Jones who stirred things up, leading to a team meeting called by Tom Glavine.

"He's no rookie," Glavine said. "He came in here a very mature player. He knows exactly what he is saying and doing."

Jones acknowledges that he loves the attention.

"I learned a long time ago that you have to be a little cocky," he said. "But you don't go overboard. You want to show your opponent that you are confident and then you back it up on the field. It's pretty simple."

Jones had earned the starting left field job before the 1994 season, but was injured late in spring training and missed the entire year after having major knee surgery. He says the injury played a part in his success this season.

"I have never worked out like I did to come back from that surgery, especially with the lower part of my body," he said. "And I think I matured mentally. It was a long wait. But it really did pay off."

In the strike-shortened season, Jones hit 23 homers and drove in 86 runs. This was while hitting behind two players, Marquis Grissom and Jeff Blauser, who did not have good seasons. He was just as solid in the 14 playoff games, when he hit .364 with three homers and eight RBIs.

In Game 1 of the divisional playoffs against the Rockies, Jones hit two homers, including one to win the game with two out in the top of the ninth inning. He also made a game-saving play in the eighth, laying out to snag a ball hit by Andres Galarraga that would have scored two runs.

Javier Lopez was solid behind the plate and at the plate, where he led the Braves with a .315 average.

Opposite page: KIMBERLY SMITH

Chipper Jones could become the next Dale Murphy, a player who thrills with his bat, glove ... and personality.

THE 1995 ATLANTA BRAVES

The Braves were patient with Mark Wohlers, turning down several trade offers over recent years.

DAVID TULIS

Bravo!

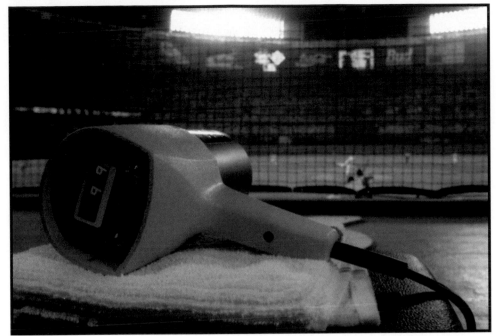

JONATHAN NEWTON

*Mark Wohlers'
fastball is
consistently in
the 99–100
mph range.*

The next night he started the game-tying rally in the ninth and the game-winning rally in the 11th. And in the final game, he doubled home two runs to cut into a 3-0 deficit, and the Braves went on to win 10-4. He hit .389 for the series.

His outstanding regular season led to strong Rookie of the Year consideration. The top contenders were Jones and Hideo Nomo of the Dodgers, who led the league in strikeouts.

"Ever since David Justice won the award in 1990 (the year Jones was drafted), I made it a goal to come out and try to win it again for the Braves," Jones said. "With L.A. winning the last three, I'd like to break that string."

Jones, who played shortstop in the minors, will be back at third base next season, but there's talk in the organization that some day he could be in the outfield, possibly in center. "I like third, but whatever they want me to do is fine," Jones said. "I can play out in the outfield just as easily."

Just as Jones stepped to the front at third base, Wohlers settled things down in the bullpen. He had been expected to take the closer's role for years, and this season the Braves' patience was finally rewarded.

When Maddux was with the Cubs in 1991, he was watching the Braves on television when he saw Wohlers for the first time. He remembers his impression of the then-21-year-old hard-throwing righthander: "Totally awesome. This guy's unbelievable. He's got a chance to be the best closer in the game."

Earlier this year, Wohlers moved his locker next to Maddux's and started picking up a little free advice. According to Maddux, the first lesson

BRAVO!

went something like this. "I can't tell you how to pitch with a 95 mph fastball, but I can tell you how to close out a ballgame. If you get two outs, the inning's not over. No matter who the pitcher is, we all start taking things for granted. You can't do that. If you realize you can't take anything for granted, your concentration will increase and you'll pitch better."

Wohlers says the main reason he moved near Maddux was to get away from pitching coach Leo Mazzone and "a lot of reporters at Leo's locker, saying, 'What the hell's wrong with Wohlers?' "

"I tried not to listen, but it was hard," Wohlers said. "I know Leo has my best interest at heart and was totally being honest. But I knew what was wrong with me and I didn't need to hear all that. I don't read the local newspapers. I don't listen to the talk shows and I still hear it. So I can imagine how bad it is."

Added his wife, Nancy, "The biggest thing he stopped doing was reading the newspaper. He just started listening to his inner feelings and own voice, not other people's opinions. He's trying to get into life. We bought a house in Alpharetta (in late '93) and he's getting into that."

Wohlers' approach on the mound changed, also. His control has always

Ryan Klesko was awesome against right-handed pitching, hitting 20 of his 23 home runs and batting .331.

JONATHAN NEWTON

Chipper Jones met an ex-president, then went out and campaigned for rookie-of-the-year votes.

been a problem. But he concentrated on his best pitch — a 100 mph fastball — going only with his offspeed pitch after setting it up with the fastball. The effect was tremendous. During one game in San Diego, the speed of each pitch was being shown on the scoreboard. On one pitch, 102 mph flashed up and the crowd couldn't believe it. Then he came back with a 83 mph slider, and the hitter almost threw the bat trying to hit it.

"I knew I had above-average major league stuff, but I was no more than an average major league pitcher," Wohlers said. "I thought, 'Enough is enough.' My ability was more than I was contributing to this team. I wasn't satisfied where my career was. I didn't want to be a set-up man for a closer. I didn't want to be average."

Bravo!

THE 1995 ATLANTA BRAVES

And Cox stayed patient with Wohlers, bringing him right back after a bad outing — a luxury he didn't have in tight pennant races the previous four seasons. Wohlers finished with 25 saves and a 2.09 ERA. He wasn't totally dominating in October, but he pitched in 11 of the 14 playoff games, going 1-1 with four saves and a 2.84 ERA.

"We couldn't afford to let guys work through slumps," Wohlers said. "That was one of the biggest keys. I was able to get back out there because of our position in the standings. Any relief pitcher, after a loss or blown save, you want to get right back in there and redeem yourself. A year or two ago, I might not have been back in there right away."

But the Braves knew his potential, and general manager John Schuerholz refused to bite as team after team made bids for Wohlers over the years.

"I was hoping, anticipating that he would make the breakthrough," Schuerholz said. "Not with any (great) numbers; he's still developing. But a breakthrough by him to be able to deal with that role productively and effectively. As an organization, we've been very patient with that development. We had to be, because of his age."

So when the season came down to one final out, when the title was about to become Atlanta's, Wohlers was on the mound. "It was awesome being out there, being able to do that," Wohlers said. "It has been a long way to that moment."

For Klesko, this was a strange but satisfying season. He started in a platoon in left field with the right-handed hitting Mike Kelly and got off to a terrible start. He didn't hit a home run in his first 56 at-bats. But despite sharing time in left even after Kelly was sent down, Klesko remained patient.

"I'm young and I know Bobby likes to work young players slowly (into fulltime roles)," Klesko said. "I realize I'm going to get my chance, and when I do, I'm going to give them something." He may get his chance next season. If the Braves don't bring back Fred McGriff, Ryan will get a chance to play every day, going back to his natural position at first base.

"I worked hard out in left and I think I can become a good outfielder. People just have to give me time," he said. "But I have always played first and I would feel more comfortable there. It's my spot."

Javier Lopez appeared more comfortable this season, especially at the plate. In Game 2 of the National League Championship Series against the Reds, he put the game away in the 10th with a three-run homer. In Game 2 of the World Series, he broke open a 2-2 game with a two-run shot off Dennis Martinez. He also made a key defensive play in that game, picking off Manny Ramirez in the eighth when he threw behind him at first.

"The whole playoffs I will never forget," Lopez said. "And that moment when it was all over and I went out to the mound and grabbed Wohlers . . . I felt about 10 feet off the ground."

FRANK NIEMEIR

BRAVO!

CHAPTER 6

THE BRAINTRUST

I T'S A GREAT PICTURE. TED TURNER, STAN KASTEN, JOHN Schuerholz and Bobby Cox, holding the World Series trophy, grinning broadly, champagne dripping from their chins.

They are the architects of the Braves' world championship. From the board room to the dugout, they have steered this team to the top of the baseball world.

They are a diverse team, both in background and personality. Before becoming involved in baseball, Kasten was a lawyer, Schuerholz a junior high school teacher, Turner a rising television magnate. Only Cox is a lifetime baseball man.

Turner's exploits as owner of the Braves are legendary. But he has moved to the background in recent years, leaving his "baseball people" to run the team. The results have been extraordinary.

The front man is Kasten, the team president. Stan is one of the best negotiators in sports and certainly one of the toughest. He loves to intimidate people, using language as foul as any heard in the clubhouse. But he's fair, and he never, ever lies to the media. He may not tell you everything you want to know, but he won't lie to you.

During last winter's labor negotiations, it became

John Schuerholz and Bobby Cox have steered the Braves to the top of the baseball world.

Stan Kasten,
John Schuerholz,
Ted Turner and
Bobby Cox are a
diverse team, both
in background
and personality.

THE 1995 ATLANTA BRAVES

clear that Kasten wields enormous power. I talked to him on a daily basis, and it was obvious that he wanted to get a deal done. But he was fighting two battles — one against the players union, another against baseball's old guard. A compromise did not seem to be a part of either's agenda.

Stan has a passion for his job. He is involved at every level, from player acquisitions to the new stadium. (The new ballpark, by the way, is his baby. He has been to all the new ones — Coors Field, Jacobs Field, Camden Yards — to see what parts he would like to incorporate in the Atlanta stadium).

Kasten's best move came in October, 1990, when he hired Schuerholz as general manager.

Schuerholz and Kasten are opposites. Even on a hot summer day,

FRANK NIEMEIR

Stan Kasten, who enjoys the media spotlight, is involved at every level of the operation, from player acquisitions to the new stadium.

Schuerholz looks as if he stepped out of a Neiman Marcus catalog. Kasten always has his sleeves rolled up, and he sweats even in the winter. Schuerholz doesn't care for the media. Kasten loves them. Schuerholz, a former English teacher, talks in complete sentences. Kasten relies on unprintable adjectives.

But this is a friendly — and powerful — relationship.

Kasten lets Schuerholz call most of the shots when it comes to putting the team together. Schuerholz does need Kasten's approval on new contracts, but rarely is he told no. When the Braves traded for Marquis Grissom last spring, Schuerholz knew Grissom's $4.9 million salary would put the Braves over their payroll budget. But he still got the OK.

*John Schuerholz
and Bobby Cox
have a strong
mutual respect.*

"I wanted to do it," Kasten said at the time, "but this is a real strain on our budget. We have diminished our flexibility. John and I almost always come to the same conclusion. It doesn't always end in what he started wanting to do ... but most of the time it does."

Schuerholz is a tough guy to get to know. He's extremely guarded and rarely lets anything slip. His lieutenants, assistant GM Dean Taylor and scouting director Paul Snyder, know that, and they're also hard to crack. But John knows baseball, and he surrounds himself with talented people. Taylor negotiates many of the contracts. Snyder, who has been with the organization since 1957, has one of the best scouting minds in the game, helping bring in players such as Chipper Jones, Tom Glavine and David Justice. Bill Lajoie is Schuerholz's front man on trades. Chuck LaMar played a key role as scouting and minor league director before taking a job as general manager of the expansion Tampa Bay Devil Rays.

Schuerholz is the one who makes it work, taking in tons of information

DAVID TULIS

"I feel most comfortable in the dugout," Bobby Cox said. *"That is where I want to be. That is where I belong."*

DAVID TULIS

BRAVO!

John Schuerholz traded for Marquis Grissom (right) during spring training, then made deals for Luis Polonia, Mike Devereaux (left) and Alejandro Peña during the season.

DAVID TULIS

DAVID TULIS

Bravo!

JONATHAN NEWTON

The players all like Bobby Cox, partly because "we know Bobby's not going to throw a tirade after a loss," says Tom Glavine.

and deciding which direction to take. Like Kasten, Schuerholz is a great negotiator. He's relentless, and he never lets a few extra dollars cost him a player. Just ask Kasten.

He's also very good at recognizing weak spots and plugging holes. Going into this season, he knew that anything less than a world title would be disappointing. So he gave up some good prospects for players to fill specific roles on the club. And the three players he brought in — Alejandro Peña, Mike Devereaux and Luis Polonia — all played a huge part in winning the championship. Without them, who knows what would have happened?

About the only thing Schuerholz and Cox have in common is that their paycheck is signed by the same person. They're even more different than Schuerholz and Kasten.

But Schuerholz lets Cox run the club on the field, never telling him which player to hit second or what pitcher to use in the ninth inning. They have a lot of mutual respect.

Until the Braves won the title, however, Schuerholz was regarded as this organization's savior and Bobby was seen as just another manager. But Cox was the one who, when he was GM of the Braves, put together the solid farm and scouting system that led to the team's current success. Cox is finally getting credit for that, and for being a capable manager, too.

He never gets too excited, but after the Series it was apparent in his voice that this was a huge step for him.

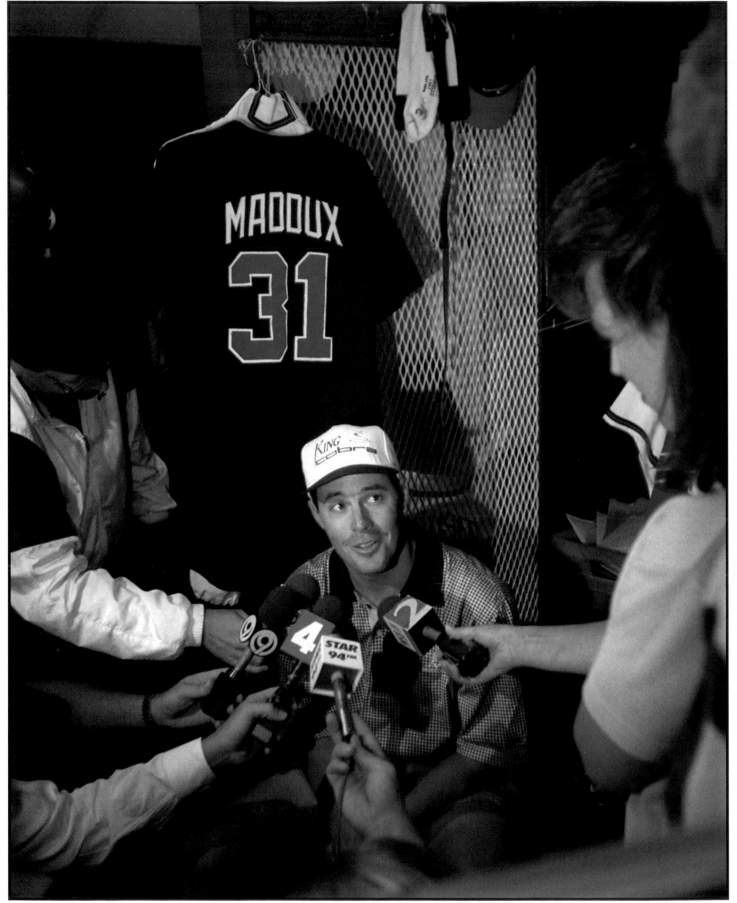

BRAVO!

CHAPTER 7

HOME AWAY FROM HOME

BASEBALL PLAYERS SPEND A LOT OF TIME AT THE BALL-park. On a typical game day, they'll arrive before 4 in the afternoon and not leave until after 11 p.m. Even with batting practice and three-hour games, that leaves a lot of free time. Much of that time is spent in the clubhouse.

They eat in the clubhouse. Sometimes they sleep in the clubhouse. They play cards, watch TV, exercise, get dressed, read, answer mail, talk, check their stocks on their cellular phones, practice their putting ... all in their home-away-from-home.

Let's take a tour of the Braves' clubhouse, locker-by-locker:

Marquis Grissom: When you walk in the door, his is one of the first lockers. Everyone calls him Grip, a nick-name that goes back to his days in Montreal. Marquis is usually pretty quiet, but he likes to talk about his family, his 14 brothers and sisters. He never, ever makes excus-es or brags about himself. He's from Atlanta, and he real-ly wants to stay here. "I thought it would be a pain get-ting tickets for everybody," he said. "But it's neat playing in my hometown. If I never leave that would be fine with me."

Greg Maddux's locker is a favorite stop for the media, though he speaks so softly he's hard to hear sometimes.

*David Justice
spends a lot of time
in the clubhouse,
talking about
everything from
world politics to
his wife's movies.*

FRANK NIEMEIR

BRAVO!

Ryan Klesko: He's as outgoing as Marquis is quiet. He loves attention from the media. He's picked up bow hunting from Charlie O'Brien and usually has a bunch of hunting clothes in his locker. Most people don't know that Ryan was a top pitching prospect in high school. He might have been one of the top two or three picks in the 1989 draft if not for a serious arm injury. That's when he started playing first base, and the Braves picked him in the sixth round. What a steal. A couple of years ago in spring training, Klesko missed the team bus to a game in Melbourne. I gave him a ride, and we talked a lot. He had a tough upbringing. His parents are divorced, and his mother had a terrible accident at the chemical factory where she worked, burning her throat. His dad lives in Atlanta, and he has medical problems, too.

David Justice: He spends a lot of time in the clubhouse, talking about everything from world politics to his wife's movies. Justice is very defensive of his race. During the O.J. Simpson case, David was the only black player on the team who was outspoken about the trial. To him, there was no way O.J. was guilty. When the verdict came down, he was very excited. There was a time when reporters had a difficult time dealing with David, but since his marriage to Halle Berry, he's become very good with the media. He still likes his privacy, though. In the offseason, he had his left nipple pierced and the paper did a short story about it. Channel 11 wanted to get a shot of the ring and sent a camera crew into the clubhouse, but when Justice came out of the shower he had a towel draped over the ring. They never got the shot.

Mike Devereaux: He loves to talk about the house he's building at the Golf Club of Georgia. "It's going to be 10,000 square feet," he said. "And it's going to be just me in the house."

Luis Polonia: Luis is a great dresser, and he likes to wear fancy sunglasses. Polonia and Devereaux, two newcomers this season, have become good friends. He's also friends with Carlos Perez, the Montreal pitcher who was arrested for allegedly raping a woman when the Expos were in town in September. The word was that Polonia had introduced Perez to the woman. When I asked about it, Polonia was really nervous. When he was with the Yankees, he had been arrested for having sex with a minor. He would only say that he and Perez "went our separate ways ... that is all I'm going to say about that."

Greg McMichael: He's one of the nicest guys in sports. He's a very religious person, and he puts together team chapel on Sundays. Greg has perhaps the biggest appetite on the team. He's always eating — before the game, after the game, on team charters, in hotel lobbies. He has become more comfortable with his role on the team since losing the closer's job.

Kent Mercker: Kent's a nice guy, but he's never been a big favorite of manager Bobby Cox. It seems like every year he produces, but in the post-

DAVID TULIS

Luis Polonia is a great dresser, and he likes to wear fancy sunglasses.

JONATHAN NEWTON

*When Jeff
Blauser's batting
average plunged,
so did his normally
cheerful attitude.*

Mark Wohlers: He's big, and sometimes he can be short with the media, but he's really a pussycat. He's bothered about the weight he's picked up over the last year, about 20 pounds. He says he'll lose it after the season, but the way he pitched maybe he ought to keep eating.

Greg Maddux: His locker is always a mess. He probably gets more fan mail than anyone on the team. But day after day, he'll sit and sign cards that young fans send him. He also likes to play cards in the clubhouse. There's often a crowd around his locker — with so many great performances, he's always in demand — but he has such a soft voice that it's hard for reporters to hear him.

Jeff Blauser: Jeff used to keep a collection of dirty pictures in his locker, and he had a fat doll that would drop its pants and squirt water on you. Over the last five years, I've spent a lot of time with Jeff, talking about everything from the stock market to religion. His locker used to be a hangout for the media, but that changed this season. When Jeff's batting average plummeted, he became a different person. He didn't want reporters hanging around. He said I was too negative about him, and said the fans just didn't understand what was going on. What was bothering Jeff was his $10 million contract. He wasn't living up to it, and he felt badly about his production.

Charlie O'Brien: His locker looks like a hunting store. Charlie is the only one in the clubhouse who goes out of his way to try to intimidate the media. The best way to handle that is to yell right back at him.

Mark Lemke: He spends a lot of time at his locker reading, and he has learned to speak Spanish fluently. Few people realize how important he is to this club. He keeps everybody loose, and there's no one on the team who doesn't like him. Don't be surprised if he finishes his career in Atlanta. Cox loves him. Earlier this year, Lemke put an X-rated photo on his locker. One day a local television crew came by to interview him. The reporter didn't notice the photo, which was right over Lemke's shoulder, and it showed up on the news that night.

Ed Giovanola: A September callup who got a spot on the World Series roster when Blauser was injured, Giovanola is learning some bad habits from Lemke. One of them is not shaving.

Pedro Borbon: His dad, Pedro Borbon Sr., pitched for the Big Red Machine, and he loves to talk about the time he spent in the Reds clubhouse as a child. One of his best friends was Ken Griffey Jr., whose father played on the team, too. "I used to fight Ken Jr. all the time," Pedro said. "And in the sixth inning we would go into the tunnel and play a pickup game until the real game was over. Sparky Anderson had a policy that kids couldn't go into the clubhouse after losses because he would be in a terrible mood. But looking back, I can remember only two times not being able to go in. That's how much they won."

Alejandro Peña: He spends a lot of time in the training room, and he keeps to himself. When he was with the Braves in '91, he was involved in a combined no-hitter with Wohlers and Mercker. He held on to the game ball after getting the last out. But on it he wrote: "Save No. 8."

Brad Clontz: He looks about 20 years older when he takes off his hat. He didn't seem comfortable in the closer's role early in the season. "Here I was going into a season with the team that has won more games than anyone else the last few years, and I'm the closer my first year in the majors," he said. "I had a lot to learn, a lot of maturing to do."

Eddie Perez: After the Carlos Perez incident, Eddie said it caused some trouble for him back home in Venezuela. "My mother sees headlines that a Perez in Atlanta has gotten in trouble," he said. "Well, she thinks it's me and calls and before I can say a word, she is screaming and everything and wondering what is going on. I finally had to put my wife on the telephone to tell her that everything was fine. She got her calmed down, but it wasn't funny." Get used to seeing Eddie around; he's going to be Lopez's backup for a long time.

Fred McGriff: He's a very quiet person, but he loves to talk about the

Mark Lemke keeps everyone loose in the clubhouse. There's no one on the team who doesn't like him.

Marquis Grissom is usually quiet in the clubhouse, but he likes to talk about the 14 brothers and sisters he grew up with in Atlanta.

DAVID TULIS

BRAVO!

JONATHAN NEWTON

John Smoltz is the best golfer on the team. He always keeps a set of clubs in the clubhouse.

Tampa Bay Buccaneers. He's from Tampa, and lives there in the offseason. Fred is a free agent, and it bothers him that the Braves made absolutely no attempt to resign him during the season.

Rafael Belliard: For years, he had a sugar bear honey dispenser in his locker. One day it was gone, and to this day no one will admit to taking it. Belliard thinks it was Blauser. Rafael is one of the most polite athletes around. He's always in a good mood.

Javier Lopez: Lopez is a hero in his hometown of Ponce, Puerto Rico. Girls are always yelling at him and Justice in airports, hotels, anywhere they go.

Pat Corrales: Pat is the only coach who plays cards with the players. He recently built a house up at Big Canoe, Ga., and loves to talk about it. He's been a manager for three different major league clubs, but he doesn't want that role again.

Jim Beauchamp: He's probably the quietest of the coaches. He makes out the lineup card every day. Poor Jim has gone through some terrible injuries with the club. One time he slipped when coming off the bus in New

Rafael Belliard is probably the most polite athlete on the team. He's always in a good mood.

MARLENE KARAS

York and had to have knee surgery. Two years ago, in St. Louis, he was hit in the face with a ball in batting practice and almost lost sight in one eye.

Clarence Jones: He spends a lot of time talking with his hitters. He's a quiet person, but very nice. He's turning into a good golfer.

Ned Yost: He's always talking about his buddy Dale Earnhardt, and he has a bunch of NASCAR junk in his locker. He's also a very good hunter and owns a local clothing store.

Leo Mazzone: He's great to be around. He always has a good joke, though everyone has heard most of them. Mazzone, like Cox, is very defensive about his pitchers. He's a much better quote than Cox, though. Cox will bend over backward to protect a pitcher who's just thrown a horrible game, but Mazzone will be more honest about the situation. Cox sometimes gets mad at him for doing that.

Bravo!

Jimy Williams: He keeps to himself, reading books and doing crossword puzzles. Of all the coaches, he knows the game best. He's Cox's right-hand man and tough to get to know.

* * *

The clubhouse is run by Casey Stevenson, with the help of the clubbies, a group of about a dozen youngsters in their late teens and early 20s who jump at the players' every request.

This is Stevenson's clubhouse. He cooks, he cleans, he keeps the uniforms and equipment in order ... and he does a great job. Casey takes his job seriously, and he doesn't cower to the millionaire ballplayers or the rookies who may someday be stars. Many times on the road I've seen a player chew out a clubbie. It's a nasty scene. But in Atlanta, they learn very quickly not to mess with Casey.

The players pay about $23 a day in clubhouse dues, for food and laundry. The players are charged for extra equipment, and the team keeps a running tab that the player must pay at the end of the season.

When a player comes to the ballpark, he pulls his car into the tunnel under the stadium, gets out and gives his keys to one of the clubbies. The clubbies park the cars, and after the game they bring them right outside the clubhouse door so the players don't have to run into fans after games.

Clubbies do the laundry, clean shoes and run errands. In return, they get tips from the players at the end of the season. Some players write big checks; some are pretty small. Former Braves Mike Stanton and Deion Sanders were notorious for being cheap with the clubhouse tips.

Stevenson also runs the umpires room, and cooks for them. (Casey and visiting team clubhouse man John Holland are great chefs. Sometimes when Casey cooks spaghetti, I get a plate. It's the best meat sauce in town.)

Holland has basically the same duties as Stevenson, but is tipped at the end of each series by the visiting team. Typically, it comes to about $125 a player. Teams with a lot of veterans tip more.

Here's a quick rundown of the clubhouse crew: Mike Hill, Chuck Armstrong and Fred Stone work for Holland in the visiting clubhouse. Paul Bodi covers the right-field line during the game. Ryan Magnon works the left-field line. Chris Ellis, known as Speedy, is the homeplate ball boy. (He's the one you can see running to the plate to give the umpire more balls.) Clint Van Zant and Craig Magnon are bat boys for the Braves dugout. Antonio Farmer wears the uniform of the other team and serves as their bat boy. Chris Van Zant helps Stevenson with the umpires room. And Kevin Banks works in the Braves clubhouse fulltime.

Casey Stevenson runs the clubhouse, with the help of the clubbies, a group of about a dozen youngsters who jump at the players' every request.

MARLENE KARAS

Bravo!

CHAPTER 8

LIFE ON THE ROAD

PERHAPS THE TOUGHEST PART OF BEING A BASEBALL player is spending so much time away from home. Including spring training, it adds up to about 143 nights on the road every year — if you could get a season without a strike, that is.

But major league ballplayers are treated like royalty on road trips. They fly on special charters, their rooms and meals are paid for, and they don't carry their own bags.

In fact, they never even touch their bags. Before the road trip, they drive underneath the stadium and a clubhouse attendant takes their bags and loads them on a truck. The next time a player sees his bags is when a bellman comes to his hotel room and plops them down on the bed.

The Braves take a Delta charter on all road trips, and the in-flight service is outstanding. Each player gets a whole row of seats if he wants. The attendants serve a huge meal, and there's an unlimited supply of oversized candy bars. Mixed drinks and beer are available, too.

Manager Bobby Cox, the coaches and the front-office types sit in first class, and the players sit toward the back. Many of the guys play cards. John Smoltz, Greg

Coors Field, the Rockies' new stadium in Denver, is the nicest park the Braves visit over the course of a season.

The players get $67.50 a day for meal money, and some of them don't easily part with it.

Maddux and Steve Avery have been locked in many intense Hearts battles.

The Braves get the same flight attendants for almost every trip. Not only do they know the players and coaches by name, they also know what each one likes to drink. Cox used to drink on the charter flights, but switched to non-alcoholic beer after the domestic violence incident with his wife last summer.

There's a lot of smoking on the flight, most of it in the first-class cabin. A few of the players light up, too. They have begged me not to use their names. "My mom would go nuts if she knew I smoked," said one player.

Everyone is pretty well behaved, especially when their wives are on the flight. There are usually a few kids running around the plane. Pat Corrales' son, Pat Jr., makes a lot of trips. He carries around a bag where he hides extra candy bars.

The food on a charter is much better than on a regular flight. They start with a snack, then have a choice of three entrees for the main meal, all with huge helpings. There's usually ice cream for dessert.

When the charter lands, the Braves don't go through the airport concourse. They exit onto the tarmac, where buses are waiting to take them to the hotel. There are always two buses. The first one is for Cox, the coaches, the support personnel and players who are with their wives. The second bus is for players only. I once made the mistake of getting on the second bus. Before I made it past the first seat, the players were screaming. Red-faced, I went to the front bus and took a seat in the fourth row. Then Corrales pointed out — quite loudly — that the first seven rows were saved for the coaches. Even more red-faced, I moved to the back of the bus.

The hotels where the team stays are nice, but not extravagant. Mostly Marriotts, Westins and Sheratons. The players don't have to check in at the front desk. Traveling secretary Bill Acree has their keys ready when they get off the bus.

Everyone in the traveling party has a single room, and Cox and general manager John Schuerholz each take a suite. Typically, the better-known players will register under fake names to avoid annoying phone calls.

Everyone in the group gets $67.50 a day for meal money, which Acree dispenses in one lump sum before the trip. It's funny, but some of these guys making millions of dollars a year don't like to part with that meal money. When Deion Sanders was with the Braves, he would do anything to save the dough, sharing a cab to the ballpark or getting a free limo ride because of his name. And he never had a problem getting a free meal at a restaurant.

And yes, there are groupies who hang out in the hotel lobby, and a few of the women qualify as major league. Remember Susan Sarandon's character in the movie *Bull Durham?* Enough said. This book is rated PG.

The Braves travel to 13 cities in the National League. Here's how I rate them, from worst to first.

MARLENE KARAS

The hotels where the Braves stay are nice, but not extravagant. John Schuerholz (left) and Bobby Cox get suites; everyone else gets a single room.

Houston: Hot. Sweaty. Humid. Flies as big as birds. That's why they play indoors at the Astrodome. But the Dome is a lousy place for baseball. It's dank, it's dirty and it smells bad. There's no ballpark atmosphere. The crowd is usually small, and half the people who do show up are pulling for the Braves. One bright spot in Houston is this old cab driver who is usually around to drive the players between the hotel and the stadium. After a game, he gives a few players a ride back to the hotel, then comes back to the stadium and waits for me to finish writing. Then he takes me somewhere to pick up dinner, and I treat him to a strawberry soda. He makes an unpleasant place bearable.

Cincinnati: Riverfront Stadium is very similar to the bucket of bolts we have in Atlanta, only it's not as well kept. They've put very little money into it since it was built in 1970. The press box is enclosed, which all the writers hate, and they keep the temperature just above freezing by running the air conditioner full blast. The visiting clubhouse is run by a man named Charlie, who every year pulls the mongoose trick on a rookie. Charlie has a cage with a grated top that you can barely see through. He ties a string to a raccoon tail and puts it in the cage, and puts the cage on a clubhouse table. At least one rookie will take the bait and go over to take a look. When the rookie gets close enough, Charlie yanks on a string and the tail comes flying out, usually sending the rookie running for cover. It's worked on a lot of players over the years, including Terry Pendleton and Marquis Grissom. "I actually climbed a locker," Grissom says. "I was scared to death."

Pittsburgh: The steel mills are long gone, and this is actually a very nice city. But Three Rivers Stadium is lousy. Like Houston, there is very little support from the city. Braves announcer Don Sutton pulled a great stunt here when he was playing for the Dodgers. Sutton was pitching in a scoreless game when manager Tommy Lasorda pulled him for a pinch hitter in the sixth inning. Sutton was furious. He wanted to leave the ballpark, but the Dodgers had a rule that no one could leave early. So Sutton went in the clubhouse, put on his baseball jacket and headed up to the Allegheny Club, a restaurant on the club level down the first-base line. Sutton ordered dinner and a bottle of wine, then had a phone brought to his table and called pitching coach Red Adams in the dugout. When Adams inquired as to his whereabouts, Sutton told him to look up the first-base line. Said Sutton, "You saw every head on the bench turn and look up at me, including Tommy's." Needless to say, Lasorda wasn't very happy. But Sutton had the last laugh. "I charged the whole meal and wine to Tommy," Sutton says.

St. Louis: There's a lot of baseball tradition here and the fans are great, regardless of whether the team is any good. Busch Stadium is one of those old round ballparks with artificial turf, but it's kept spotless and the view of the Great Arch is impressive. The players don't like it, though, because the stadium is only a few blocks from the team hotel. Autograph seekers know this, and the players sometimes have to walk well out of their way to avoid being mobbed. If they don't, the crush of fans can be incredible.

Miami: Joe Robbie Stadium is in the middle of nowhere. It's really a football stadium, and it gets incredibly hot here during the summer. But the team stays at a great hotel in Ft. Lauderdale, and the players spend a lot of time by the pool. A lot of the guys bring golf clubs on this trip, and most of them have contacts at the local courses because they play here during spring training. There's a ping pong table in the clubhouse that's a big hit.

Philadelphia: If you want a great cheese steak, this is the place to be. But there's nothing tougher than getting a cab out of Veterans Stadium after a game. Still, the players love it because there's pizza in the clubhouse before the game. This is a great newspaper town; the Inquirer and the Daily News have very good sports sections.

New York: There's a lot of traffic and the cabbies usually don't speak a lick of English, but everyone likes coming here for a few days. The team stays at the Grand Hyatt over Central Station and usually everyone goes out after games. Some players who don't want to wait for the team bus to the stadium will take the subway. It's an interesting, smelly ride through Manhattan and Queens to Shea Stadium. Shea has a great scoreboard in right field, but that's about the only good thing about the place.

Montreal: Everyone hates going through customs, and the hotel is not one of the best. But what a beautiful city! Mark Lemke and Jeff Blauser like to visit a small diner run by a French family near the hotel. Olympic Stadium is a mess. The retractable roof, which looks like a big rubber glove, stays closed. The Montreal Gazette is the only English-language newspaper in town. The reporters for the three French dailies write anything they want about the team, because the players can't read French. There's an awesome food court here.

Los Angeles: Dodger Stadium is the nicest facility in the league. They mop and clean up the concourse after every game, and everyone who works here is always smiling. The weather is usually perfect, and the ballpark is usually full (though the crowd is typically late arriving). After one game here, Furman Bisher, our legendary columnist, and I were waiting for a cab when Tommy Lasorda came out of the stadium and offered us a ride. This was in 1993, when his team was out of the race and the Braves and Giants were in a great struggle for the division title. Tommy had a Lincoln Town Car, and he popped on some big band music and off we went. He said he would give anything for a chance to knock the Giants out of the race on the last day of the season. (The Giants had done the same to the Dodgers two years before.)

"I hate those guys," Lasorda said. "It would make my year to knock them down." That's exactly what happened — the Braves and Giants went into the last day tied for first, and the Braves beat the Rockies and the Dodgers whipped the Giants. Lasorda got his wish.

San Diego: Whether you come here in April or July, it's always sunny and 70 degrees and everyone is wearing shorts. A great place.

Denver: Everyone should be so lucky as to get a trip to Coors Field. What a place! The atmosphere in the ballpark and on streets surrounding it is electric. This town is in love with baseball. The first two seasons, they packed 70,000 folks in Mile High Stadium. Now Coors Field is open, and it's fantastic. There's a microbrewery inside the stadium (no Budweiser served here), and dozens of shops and bars surround the ballpark. If the Braves' new stadium is as well done as this, Atlantans are in for a treat.

San Francisco: Candlestick Park is cold, windy and dirty, but the city makes up for it. Everyone loves this trip because there is so much to do after the game. Many of the players' wives make this trip and come home with bags of clothes. The area around the Parc 55 hotel is full of porno shops. Almost every player who comes here for the first time is spotted in one of those shops.

Chicago: There's no place like Wrigley Field. It's what baseball is all about. There's a manually operated out-of-town scoreboard. There are bleacher seats in the outfield, and it's always crowded out there. The park only holds about 30,000, and there's really not a bad seat in the house. It's incredible how close to the field you can get in the box seats. And Harry Caray's "Take Me Out to the Ball Game" in the middle of the seventh inning is a classic. Most of the games here are played during the day, so the players can go out at night. This is an easy place to get in trouble.

JONATHAN NEWTON

On charter flights, Bobby Cox and the coaches sit up front; the players sit farther back.

CHAPTER 9

SLUGGING THE ROCKIES

THE BRAVES WERE WORRIED GOING INTO THEIR PLAYOFF opener against the Rockies, and not just because of the new best-of-five format for the first round.

Atlanta was a heavy favorite — the Braves had beaten the Rockies 30 of 36 previous games — but the mood in the visitors clubhouse at Coors Field was hardly cocky.

"This series was feared by everyone on our team," John Smoltz said after it was over. "The Rockies are a mirror image of where we were in 1991."

The Braves, along with just about everyone else in baseball, were also worried about the new format. Playoff series have been best-of-seven since 1985, and most people didn't understand the change.

"I don't think it should be reviewed, I think it should be scuttled," said Braves general manager John Schuerholz. Manager Bobby Cox was similarly miffed. "When I saw the first round was a best-of-five, I said 'No way.' You play 162 games (144 this season) and then you grind down to five games?"

The Braves were also displeased that, even though they had homefield advantage, the first two games would be in Colorado. The Rockies could expect a big boost from the raucous crowds and thin air at Coors Field, where they hit 134 of their league-leading 200 home runs.

Fred McGriff KO'd Colorado with two home runs in Game 4.

Opposite page: MARLENE KARAS

Still, the Braves appeared to have the edge because of their pitching. Atlanta's starters for the first three games — Greg Maddux, Tom Glavine and John Smoltz — combined to win 47 games in the regular season.

But the Braves' fears turned out to be well-founded. The Rockies lost the series in four games, but not before throwing a scare into the Braves.

Game 1: Braves 5, Rockies 4

This game was supposed to belong to Maddux. But the Cy Young Award winner struggled, and a couple of young third basemen stole the spotlight.

The Braves took a 1-0 lead in the third inning on a home run by Marquis Grissom, who would go on to hit safely in all 14 postseason games. But Maddux gave up three runs in the fourth, two on a homer by former Brave Vinny Castilla. The Braves had not protected Castilla, then a shortstop, in the 1993 expansion draft. Colorado made him one of its last selections and

Game 1: Chipper Jones was the hero, hitting two home runs and making a great defensive play in the eighth.

THE 1995 ATLANTA BRAVES

MARLENE KARAS

BRAVO!

moved him to third base. He hit .309 with 32 homers and 90 RBIs in '95 and made the All-Star team.

"I always thought he was going to be a guy who would hit 18-20 home runs, drive in 80 runs, and play an OK shortstop in the big leagues," said Cox. "But I didn't think he'd be a 35 (homers), 100 (RBIs) guy."

(One reason the Braves let Castilla go is because Jeff Blauser was coming off a good season. Think how good the Braves' offense would have been this season with Castilla at short instead of Blauser, who struggled to a .211 average.)

Castilla had the spotlight early, but Braves rookie Chipper Jones, a former minor-league teammate of Castilla's, had it all to himself late.

In the sixth inning, Jones hit a solo homer to cut the Rockies' lead to 3-2. And with the Braves clinging to a 4-3 lead in the eighth, he made the defensive play of the game. The Rockies had runners at first and third and none out, and Andres Galarraga ripped a ball down the third-base line that looked like a sure double. But Jones, his body parallel to the ground, snagged it for an out. The Rockies still got one run in the inning to tie the game, but Jones' play saved a big inning.

"He definitely turned the tide," Rockies manager Don Baylor said. "That's one run in, maybe two, with a man on second and no one out."

Jones hurt his left knee on the play, the same knee that kept him out the entire 1994 season after major surgery. But it didn't take him long to shake it off — he came up in the ninth and blasted another ball over the wall to put the Braves back on top, 5-4.

"It would have to have been hanging by a thread for me to come out of there," he said of his injured knee.

The last three outs of the game were a challenge. The Rockies loaded the bases with one out against Mark Wohlers, and the Braves had to wonder if this would be a repeat of years past when the bullpen broke their hearts.

Galarraga stepped up with another chance to drive in runs. But he swung at a couple of bad pitches, then went down on a high fastball. Unfortunately for the Rockies, the pitcher was due up next — and because of all his moves earlier in the game, Baylor was out of pinch-hitters. He had to call on his best hitting pitcher, Game 2 starter Lance Painter, to face the hard-

Game 1: Greg Maddux and Mark Wohlers struggled, but the Braves escaped with a 5-4 win.

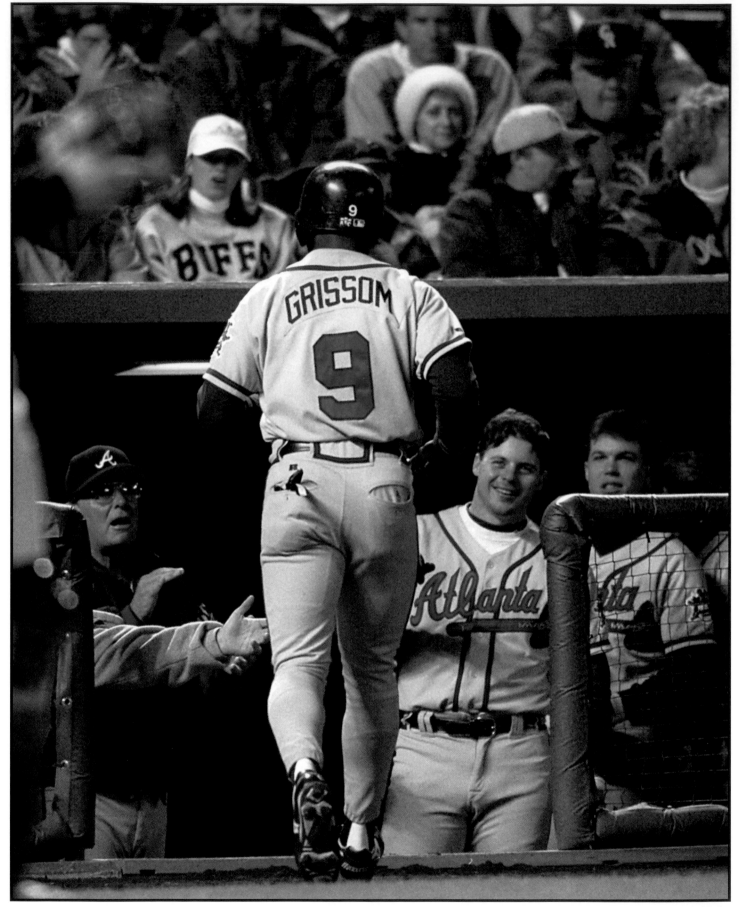

MARLENE KARAS

Bravo!

DAVID TULIS

Game 2: Tom Glavine couldn't hold a three-run lead, and Steve Avery got the call in relief.

Game 2: Marquis Grissom got a warm welcome after the second of his two home runs.

MARLENE KARAS

"It was sort of weird, but the dugout was so cool that inning, everybody knowing we were going to win," said Mark Lemke. "That feeling carried us a long way. Maybe we didn't quite have that in past Octobers."

Jones led off by ripping a ball to left for a double — his third hit of the night — and he scored on a bloop single by Fred McGriff. With two out, Mike Mordecai, in his first at-bat of the postseason, lined a ball up the middle for the lead. The Braves scored two more in the inning on a throwing error by second baseman Eric Young, and this time Wohlers shut the Rockies down easily.

In the clubhouse, the Braves seemed relieved. Even Cox, usually not one to admit anything his team does is lucky, said, "These games could have

DAVID TULIS

gone either way. They could be up 2-0 as well as us. We have gotten some breaks."

The Rockies were crushed. "We beat ourselves," Baylor said. "Not making plays, letting them get bloop hits here and there. We don't make the plays and they took advantage."

The Braves were eager to get home, but were unable to leave for Atlanta after the game because of Hurricane Opal, which was pounding the Southeast. Instead, they left the next day. That gave them a chance to see the morning papers in Denver, and the reviews of the home team were not kind. Wrote Bob Kravitz of the Rocky Mountain News: "They will never beat the Atlanta Braves. Not when it counts, not when they need to win. It could be 1993 or 1995 or 2008."

Braves announcer Don Sutton also got a feeling for the newspaper business on the trip to Denver and found he didn't like it one bit. He had agreed to write a column for the Journal-Constitution during the playoffs, and the first two were really good. As a 300-game winner with 23 years in the majors, he had great insight.

But part of his column after Game 2 was picked up by the Colorado papers and ran there the day after the game.

"My definition of paranoia probably would be what is going through the head of a pitcher in the Colorado bullpen," Sutton wrote. "That's not to put them down, but you know playing on this ballclub you can go out there, have a good inning and then you still stand a good chance of getting pulled. That's the way their manager, Don Baylor, has used it."

Baylor was furious. Sutton was embarrassed, and he decided to call it quits. He speaks his mind pretty freely on the air, but it was different for him seeing his critical words in print.

In Atlanta, rain from Opal had soaked the ground, but the tarp was out and the field was in fine shape.

Game 3: Rockies 7, Braves 5

How loose were the Rockies going into this game? "It's official, we've dug ourselves a hole," Walker said. "It's really deep. One leg is all the way through to China and all we can do is climb out."

The Rockies' nothing-to-lose attitude seemed to work. They came out swinging against John Smoltz and jumped to a 3-0 lead. The Braves came back to tie, but the Rockies went right back on top with a two-run homer by Castilla in the sixth.

Game 2: Jeff Blauser and Ryan Klesko took a tumble in left, but Marquis Grissom was there to help.

The Braves scored once in the seventh (RBI by Mordecai) and once in the ninth (RBI by Polonia) to tie it up, and the home crowd roared as the fans began to sense a sweep. But this time the bullpen struggled, allowing two runs in the 10th, and the Rockies pulled out a win. The Braves' lead in the series was down to 2-1, and the Rockies were left to wonder "what if" — though they wouldn't admit it. "Maybe just a flash goes through your mind that this could have been your third win, but that isn't reality," said Baylor.

Game 4: Braves 10, Rockies 4

If nothing else, the Colorado victory in Game 3 forced the Braves to use Maddux again, meaning he would be unavailable to start Game 1 of the NLCS against the Reds. That appeared to be a moot point early on, when Dante Bichette quieted the Atlanta crowd with a three-run blast over the right-field wall for a 3-0 Colorado lead.

But the Braves snapped out of their funk and stopped the nail-biting with four runs in the fourth, two on a double by Jones and two on a home run by McGriff. The offense got rolling — McGriff added

MARLENE KARAS

Game 3: The Rockies came out swinging against John Smoltz and scored three quick runs, the first when Eric Young beat a throw to Smoltz at the plate after a wild pitch.

MARLENE KARAS

BRAVO!

another homer and Grissom went five-for-five — and the Braves breezed to an easy win.

Amid a somewhat subdued celebration, the Braves were happy to see the Rockies get out of town. "I'm glad we don't have to come back and play them," McGriff said. "They came into this series with nothing to lose and they played us hard."

Said Grissom, "You never know what might have happened tomorrow night. They might have jumped to an early lead; we might have panicked. I'm glad it's over."

But the Braves had to wonder if they were ready for the Cincinnati Reds, who had blasted the Dodgers out of the playoffs in three straight. Atlanta's starters had a 4.38 ERA in the series with the Rockies and Maddux had allowed seven runs in 14 innings.

Game 4: Ryan Klesko had a few choice words for a Rockies pitcher. In the end, Javier Lopez was all smiles.

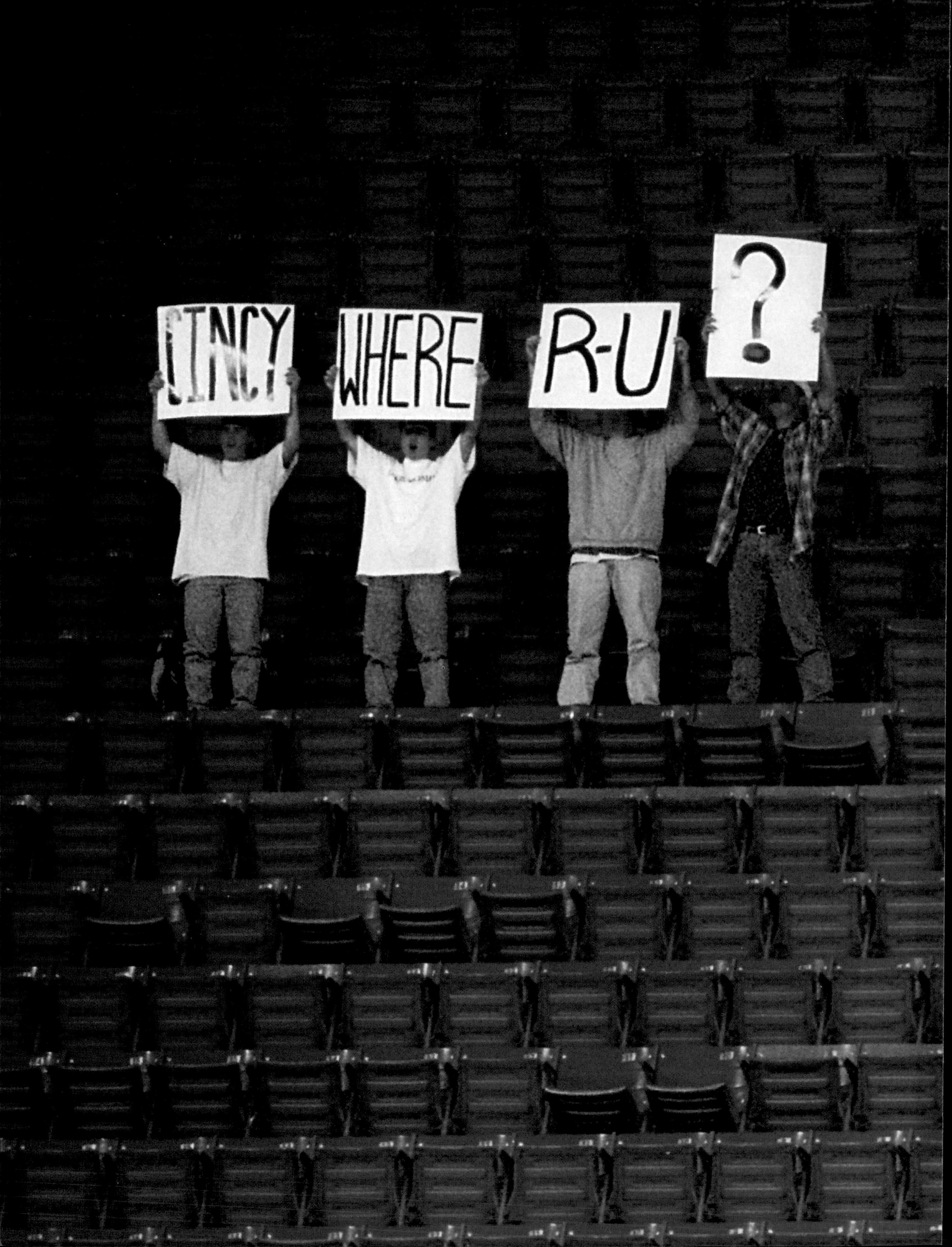
CINCY
WHERE
R-U
?

CHAPTER 10

SWEEPING THE REDS

THE REDS SHOULD HAVE KNOWN THEY WERE IN TROUBLE as soon as they took the field for Game 1 of the National League Championship Series. The much-anticipated showdown with the Braves was only minutes away, and the upper deck at Riverfront Stadium was as deserted as downtown Atlanta at high noon on Sunday.

Cincinnati had been looking forward to this meeting all season, especially after the Braves came into Riverfront and swept three games in mid-September. Atlanta and Cincinnati had the best records in the National League, and the winner of this matchup would be favored to win the World Series.

"It's like two trains heading toward each other on the same track," said Ron Gant, the former Brave. "There's going to be a big collision, and hopefully we're going to be the team that comes out with the least wreckage."

Someone must have forgotten, however, to tell the Reds fans. Only 36,372 showed up for the opener — leaving 16,190 empty seats.

But maybe they knew something. The anticipated drama never developed. The Braves swept the series in four games, dominating the Reds with outstanding pitching, timely hitting and great play from their bench.

There were more than 16,000 empty seats for Game 1 in Cincinnati.

Opposite page: JONATHAN NEWTON

Game 1: Pete
Schourek carried
a 1-0 lead into
the ninth, having
allowed the Braves
just four hits.

Game 1: Braves 2, Reds 1 (11 innings)

The Reds had figured out the perfect scenario for this series: their left-handed starters would shut down the lefthanded hitters in the middle of the Braves' order, and the Reds' offense would scratch out just enough runs to win. Pete Schourek, who won 18 games in the regular season, followed that script to perfection in the opener — and the Reds lost anyway.

Schourek carried a 1-0 lead into the ninth inning, having allowed just four hits and not letting a single Brave move past first base. But just as they had all season, the Braves battled back.

Chipper Jones led off the ninth with a single and raced to third on Fred McGriff's single to right. David Justice followed with a grounder to second that allowed Jones to score the tying run, and Schourek's great outing was wasted.

Mark Wohlers came on and held the Reds scoreless in the ninth and 10th, striking out four of the six hitters he faced. The Braves forged ahead in the 11th when McGriff drew a walk from Mike Jackson, went to second on a bunt by Luis Polonia and scored on a single by Mike Devereaux.

But the Reds did not go easily. Wohlers was spent after two innings, so Braves manager Bobby Cox called on Brad Clontz. The leadoff hitter, Thomas Howard, promptly doubled and went to third on a groundout by Barry Larkin.

After Steve Avery walked Mariano Duncan, Cox went to the bullpen one more time, hoping Greg McMichael could induce a double-play grounder from Reggie Sanders. The Reds had already hit into four double plays, and Sanders made it five. He grounded a ball up the middle, and Rafael Belliard grabbed it, stepped on second and threw to first to end the game.

"Yeah, we probably stole one," said Braves starter Tom Glavine. "But it's true to our form. We just don't give up, we don't give in. We may have looked feeble out there at times. But come the eighth, ninth inning, these guys know how to get the job done."

Game 2: Braves 6, Reds 2

Again the Reds battled, but again they came up short late in the game. Starters John Smoltz and John Smiley fought to a 2-2 standoff before turning it over to the relievers. The Braves' bullpen succeeded; the Reds' failed.

In the Reds' half of the eighth, Larkin doubled off Alejandro Peña and stole third when Peña didn't hold him close. The heart of the Reds' order — Gant, Sanders and Benito Santiago — was coming up, but Peña was up to the task. He got Gant to pop out behind second, then he struck out Sanders and Santiago.

The Reds threatened again in the ninth, but again the Braves' bullpen came through. Cincinnati got Jeff Branson to second base with one out, but McMichael wiggled off the hook.

The Braves finally made their move in the 10th. Reds manager Davey

DAVID TULIS

Game 1: Hal Morris upended Jeff Blauser, but not before he threw to first for one of five double plays by the Braves.

*Game 1: Mike
Devereaux
delivered the
game-winning
hit in the top
of the 11th inning.*

THE 1995 ATLANTA BRAVES

Game 2: John Smoltz kept the Braves close, and Javier Lopez's home run wrapped it up in the top of the 10th.

JONATHAN NEWTON

Johnson was out of relievers and had to bring in Mark Portugal, a starter during the season. Bad move. Two singles sandwiched around a walk loaded the bases with one out, and Portugal uncorked a wild pitch to allow Mark Lemke to score the go-ahead run. One out later, Javier Lopez put the game away with a towering three-run homer that hit the foul pole in left.

"I knew it was out, but I didn't know if it would be fair," Lopez said. "So I stood and watched it. When I saw that fair ball, it was the happiest day of my life."

Cox was downright giddy after the game. When he came into the lobby

Opposite page: DAVID TULIS

BRAVO!

Game 3: Dwight Smith wowed the crowd with the national anthem, and the Braves soon had the Reds on the run.

outside the Braves' clubhouse, he grabbed his wife Pam and kissed her. When he got to his office, he was so excited he looked as if he would start dancing. "I'm so proud of these guys," he said. "What a comeback, what a comeback. They never gave up. They just kept pounding."

In the clubhouse, the players were just as excited. They were heading back to Atlanta just two wins away from a trip to the Series.

"That's a great win," Smoltz said. "We just keep winning the close ones. We've played five games in the postseason that people say could have gone either way. Now, it's finally going our way."

In the Cincinnati clubhouse, Johnson realized his team's predicament. "There's a lot of baseball to be played, but this is a very uncomfortable position," he said.

Said Larkin, "I'm sure that it will be reported that this is over. But this team has been resilient all year. Now we have to look at it as we have nothing to lose."

All they had left to lose were two more games.

THE 1995 ATLANTA BRAVES

DAVID TULIS

Game 3: Former Brave Ron Gant let out a yell when he was hit by a pitch, but his bat stayed quiet.

BRAVO!

DAVID TULIS

Game 3: When it was over, Fred McGriff and Chipper Jones knew they needed just one more win to reach the Series.

Game 3: Braves 5, Reds 2

Playoff fever was back at Atlanta-Fulton County Stadium. The place was packed, and the home crowd was already anticipating a sweep. But for five innings the Braves faithful had little to cheer about. Greg Maddux and David Wells, a lefthander the Braves hadn't seen since the 1992 World Series when he pitched for Toronto, were locked in a scoreless duel.

It was Charlie O'Brien who sent the packed house into a frenzy, belting a three-run homer in the sixth. Whatever life the Reds had left quickly faded, and the Braves coasted the rest of the way.

"This is what you dream about ever since you're a little kid," said O'Brien. "Growing up in Oklahoma, I played Johnny Bench in the backyard. I even wore his number. I tried to hit like him, too, but that didn't work out too good."

Maddux pitched seven scoreless innings before giving up a run in the eighth. His strong outing answered a lot of the criticism about his postseason performance. "I know there's a lot of stuff written, that my postseason numbers don't look good," he said. "But what's really good is we're up 3-0. One more win and we're going to the World Series. That feels better than trying to prove something wrong."

With the comfort of a 3-0 edge, Cox made a decision to change the rotation, going with Avery in Game 4 so the three other starters could get their regular rest if they had to pitch again in this series. Before the game, Avery said he appreciated Cox's confidence. "That's why he is such a good manager," Avery said. "That's why players like to play for him. He doesn't give up on you. I know my season wasn't good, but now I get a chance to make up for some of it."

Game 4: Braves 6, Reds 0

It was no contest. Cincinnati's Big Dead Machine was finished. Avery pitched six scoreless innings and Devereaux, inserted late in the game because of an injury to Justice, put it away with a three-run homer in the seventh.

In the clubhouse, owner Ted Turner joined the party. Dripping champagne, he said, "Clutch hitting, good pitching and good defense. You've got to have everything. Like we did in this series."

General manager John Schuerholz yelled, "This is what it is all about."

Devereaux was named Most Valuable Player of the series. Of his home run, he said, "It was the most incredible feeling. It was a feeling of ... trying to realize where I was, what I had done, what the score was."

One of the last players out of the clubhouse was Avery. "You can only be kicked so long," he said. "I pride myself on being a pretty tough guy. It's been a pretty tough year. It's really satisfying for me to get off the ground and help the team."

As Glavine picked up his coat and headed for the door, he said, "Now it's time to complete this thing, to bring this town a title."

The sweep left the Braves with almost a week off before the World Series, so they got a chance to see the Indians and Mariners battle in Games 5 and 6 of the American League playoff series. They made it clear they would rather face the Indians — and not just to avoid tough Mariners lefthander Randy Johnson.

"We want to play the best in baseball," Justice said. "The Indians won 100 games. That's who we want."

He got his wish.

Game 4: With a three-game lead, Bobby Cox went with Steve Avery, and the lefthander responded with six shutout innings.

132

MARLENE KARAS

MARLENE KARAS

BRAVO!

NLCS celebration: Mark Wohlers and Javier Lopez rehearsed for the World Series; Ted Turner hoisted the trophy; and Mike Devereaux celebrated the MVP award.

MARLENE KARAS

MARLENE KARAS

CHAPTER 11

SILENCING THE INDIANS

IN THE BEGINNING, THERE WAS PITCHING. AND IN THE END, there was more pitching, and nothing else really mattered.

Not the Cleveland Indians' swaggering, potent lineup, the one with 207 regular-season home runs and the highest team batting average in 50 years.

Not the Braves' recent history of World Series failures, or the pressure they felt to win a championship.

Not David Justice's well-intentioned rip of Atlanta fans.

Not even the political incorrectness of the nicknames of the teams in baseball's national showcase.

What mattered were the bookend masterpieces by Atlanta's Greg Maddux and Tom Glavine, two pitching performances that stand among the greatest in World Series annals.

Maddux pitched a two-hitter in the opening game, a magical, masterful performance that baffled the Indians and set the tone for the Series. Glavine, incredibly, did him one better in Game 6, blanking the Indians on one hit to give Atlanta its first world championship.

The Braves, with the best record in baseball over the past five seasons, finally had the stamp of greatness.

Atlanta fans witnessed two great pitching performances, by Greg Maddux in Game 1 and by Tom Glavine in Game 6.

Opposite page: ERIC WILLIAMS

JONATHAN NEWTON

JONATHAN NEWTON

Game 1 festivities: Darius Rucker of Hootie and the Blowfish sings the national anthem; Cal Ripken Jr. throws out the first pitch; and 4-year-old Jim Jim Hassell seeks an autograph.

MARLENE KARAS

BRAVO!

As the Braves prepared for the Series, they didn't hide the pressure they felt to win the title. "There's a feeling that the team of the '90s has to win the World Series," John Smoltz said. "This is the time we have to do it. We need to win the World Series to ultimately prove our worth."

The Braves were favored, even though the Indians had won 10 more games in the regular season. Atlanta had ripped through the League Championship Series in four games, and the Braves were battled-tested, with nine players still on the team since their playoff run began in 1991, and 16 players with postseason experience. The Indians, meanwhile, had not been to the Fall Classic since 1954, and had not won it since '48, when they beat the Boston Braves.

Game 1: Braves 3, Indians 2

Maddux so completely befuddled the Indians that catcher Sandy Alomar was left to wonder if some mystical force was at work on the mound at Atlanta-Fulton County Stadium.

"The ball is there, and then it's not there," Alomar said. "I've never seen anything like it."

Neither had the rest of the Indians, who managed only two soft singles against Maddux. The Braves' righthander threw just 95 pitches, and of the 30 batters he faced, only four hit the ball out of the infield. If not for Braves errors, the Indians would have been shut out. Both of their runs were unearned.

"I don't think you'll ever see anyone pitch better than you saw Maddux pitch tonight," Indians manager Mike Hargrove said. "He just dominated the game."

The Braves got only three hits themselves, including a monster home run by Fred McGriff off Orel Hershiser in the second. Atlanta got two more runs in the seventh, one scoring on a fielder's choice by Luis Polonia, the other on a suicide squeeze by Rafael Belliard.

"I'm not a big hitter, but I can do little things," Belliard said.

JONATHAN NEWTON

Game 1: Greg Maddux held the Indians, the best-hitting team in 50 years, to two soft singles.

Game 1: Fred McGriff's long home run off Orel Hershiser in the second inning tied the game at 1-1.

FRANK NIEMEIR

Game 1: Kenny Lofton's speed led to the Indians' runs, both of which were unearned.

Still, the Indians stayed in the game because of their speed and the Braves' sloppy fielding. In the first inning, Belliard booted a grounder by leadoff hitter Kenny Lofton, who quickly stole two bases — the first time an American League player had done that since Babe Ruth (yes, Babe Ruth) in 1921. Lofton then came home on a groundout.

The Indians got one more in the ninth, thanks again to Lofton's speed. He singled with one out, and was running on the pitch when the next batter grounded to second. Lofton never slowed down, and McGriff threw the ball away when he tried to catch Lofton at third, allowing him to score. Atlanta's lead was down to one run.

But Maddux ended the game by getting Carlos Baerga to foul out to Chipper Jones, and the Braves had won the opener.

In the clubhouse, pitching coach Leo Mazzone sat with a grin on his face.

Game 1: When umpire Bruce Froeming called Mike Devereaux out at second, Bobby Cox came out to disagree.

MARLENE KARAS

Game 2: Javier Lopez hit a two-run homer to break the tie, then picked off Manny Ramirez at first base to snuff an Indians rally (following page).

Game 2: Ted Turner and Jane Fonda whooped it up as the Braves took the lead.

"I kept hearing the last couple of days people asking whether Greg is the same pitcher during the postseason as he is in the regular season," Mazzone said. "That's a ridiculous thought. I guess they won't be asking that anymore."

Maddux said he benefited from a talk with his brother Mike, who pitches for Boston and had faced the Indians in the first round of the playoffs. "Our scouting report agreed with everything he told me," Maddux said. "That helped me feel comfortable. You have to learn to live and deal with the pressure. I was a mess in Colorado, better in Cincinnati and even better here. I thought this was fun."

Game 2: Braves 4, Indians 3

Javier Lopez was doing a lot of heavy thinking as he stood at the plate, facing a 1-2 pitch from Dennis Martinez in the bottom of the sixth inning with David Justice on third base and the score tied 2-2.

"He's got Justice on third and I'm thinking he's not going to give me a curveball in the dirt. He could throw it in the dirt and have a wild pitch and

DAVID TULIS

THE 1995 ATLANTA BRAVES

Game 2: Tom Glavine held the Indians to two runs over six innings before turning it over to the bullpen.

the run would score," Lopez said, recounting his thought process. "So I'm thinking he's going to try to surprise me with a fastball away or in. I was trying to be aggressive on the pitch. The next one was a fastball away, and I took advantage of it."

He took advantage of it by blasting it over the centerfield fence to give the Braves a 4-2 lead.

But why was Martinez even pitching to Lopez, with Belliard and Glavine due up next? Lopez had never faced Martinez before, but he was hitting .391 in the postseason. Belliard was at .150 for the postseason, and had a career .174 mark against Martinez. Afterward, Hargrove would only say, "I thought he could get him out."

"I was trying to go around him a little bit," Martinez said, "but then I got two strikes and I was looking for the strikeout pitch."

Lopez was not finished with his heroics, however. After the Indians had

Game 2: Mark Wohlers pulled down the save by getting the final four outs.

MARLENE KARAS

Game 3: John Smoltz lasted only into the third inning before Bobby Cox came with the hook.

DAVID TULIS

Bravo!

closed the gap to 4-3, he short-circuited an Indians rally in the eighth by picking off Manny Ramirez with a rifle throw to first base.

"Earlier in the game, I had told Javy that Ramirez was taking real big leads at first," McGriff said. "He just decided to throw, and I happened to be there."

Glavine held the Indians to two runs in six innings, and Lopez's homer in the bottom of the sixth came just in time to make Glavine the winning pitcher. After Lopez's pickoff of Ramirez, Mark Wohlers came on to get the final four outs for a save.

Maddux, Glavine and the Braves' bullpen had combined to limit the Indians to eight hits in 64 at-bats (a .125 average) through the first two games. "One thing this pitching staff has always tried to do is be the aggressor," Glavine said. "We realize what the Indians have done and respect their numbers. At the same time, we have a lot of confidence in what we can do. We're going to go after people, attack and attack smart."

The Braves left for Cleveland knowing that they had history on their side.

Game 3: Ryan Klesko hit the first of his three home runs in the Series.

Game 4: Bobby Cox was criticized for starting Steve Avery, but he responded with six shutout innings.

JONATHAN NEWTON

BRAVO!

Of the 42 teams that had won the first two games of the World Series, 32 of them (76 percent) had gone on and taken the title.

Game 3: Indians 7, Braves 6

The Indians left Alanta in a huff, with Lofton claiming his team would have won the first two games had they been played in Cleveland. The enthusiastic home field crowd, he reasoned, was all the Indians needed to put them over the top in close games.

In Game 3, he was right.

Buoyed by the charged atmosphere at Jacobs Field, the Indians broke out their bats, pounded out 12 hits and edged the Braves in 11 innings.

"We're back," Lofton said, "but we still have a long ways to go."

The highlight of the game was the show put on by the two hard-throwing closers. Wohlers and Jose Mesa matched each other fastball for fastball from the eighth through the 10th, firing 100 mph heaters past opposing hitters for almost three innings.

But Cox had to pull Wohlers after the 10th and go with Alejandro Peña, who gave up a leadoff double to Baerga. One out later, Eddie Murray drove home pinch-runner Alvaro Espinoza with a single to center. It was the 46th time in Series history that a game ended with the winning run scoring on the final pitch.

Game 4: Braves 5, Indians 2

Cox selected Steve Avery as his Game 4 starter rather than coming back with Maddux on three days' rest. The "experts" thought he had it all wrong. Why would he leave his Cy Young winner on the bench? The second-guessing was loud and long.

But Avery made his manager look smart, pitching six scoreless innings, and the bullpen turned to an unlikely hero to close it out as the Braves moved within one win of the championship.

The game ended with Pedro Borbon — who had not pitched since Game 3 of the first round — on the mound for the final three outs. When Mazzone called the bullpen to see if Wohlers could pitch the ninth, Wohlers grabbed the phone himself and said he was ready. He wasn't. Obviously tired from his long outing the previous night, Wohlers gave up a long leadoff home run to Ramirez and a double to Paul Sorrento. But Borbon came on and got three quick outs — including two strikeouts — for the save.

"To tell you the truth, I have been thinking about this moment for a long time," said Borbon. "I knew it was going to come. I just didn't know when."

Game 5: Indians 5, Braves 4

The Mighty Casey of pitchers struck out.

Maddux, even with the benefit of an extra day's rest, just didn't have it. He spotted the Indians a 2-0 lead in the first when Albert Belle took him deep. The Braves tied it in the fifth off Orel Hershiser, but Maddux gave two runs right back in the sixth. It was 5-2 going to the ninth, and Ryan

Game 3: The Indians' victory was the 46th game in Series history to end with the winning run scoring on the final pitch.

JONATHAN NEWTON

Game 4: Ryan Klesko belted another home run, and Pedro Borbon came on to shut down the Indians in the ninth.

Klesko's long two-run homer off Mesa wasn't enough.

The Indians had altered their approach to hitting against Maddux, and were swinging early in the count. For one of the few times this year, Maddux couldn't adjust. He initiated the first physical confrontation of the Series when, after giving up the home run to Belle, he threw a ball right under the chin of Murray. Murray started toward the mound and the benches cleared, but no punches were thrown ... though the incident did seem to fire up the Indians and their fans.

The Indians tried a little gamesmanship afterward, hoping to get the Braves to think about their past Series failures.

"I think the pressure is on them," Hershiser said. "They've lost the last two World Series they've been in. Atlanta fans are probably wondering what's going on."

About 1,000 Atlanta fans were waiting at the airport when the Braves arrived home about 2:30 the next morning, chopping and cheering as the players walked through the concourse.

JONATHAN NEWTON

THE 1995 ATLANTA BRAVES

Game 5: Greg Maddux was not nearly effective as he had been in Game 1, giving up a two-run homer to Albert Belle in the first inning.

FRANK NIEMEIR

BRAVO!

Game 6: Braves 1, Indians 0

Rain forced the Braves indoors for their workout the day before the game, and the players had plenty of time to talk with reporters. It was obviously something was bothering Justice. As a small group of reporters gathered around, he started talking about the Atlanta fans. He felt they were not being supportive enough.

"If we don't win, they'll probably burn our houses down," he said. "We've got to win. And if we win, it's for the 25 guys in here, the coaches and Bobby. It is for us. Like the song '(You and Me) Against the World.' It's us against the world. I'm the only guy that will sit here and say it, but there are a lot of people who feel that way."

Justice wouldn't stop.

"If we get down 1-0 tonight, they will probably boo us out of the stadium. You would have to do something great to get them out of their seats. Shoot, up in Cleveland, they were down three runs in the ninth inning and they were still on their feet."

Then he took a shot at Hershiser: "For Orel to say there's more pressure

Game 5: Mike Mordecai was dejected after being doubled off first.

Game 6: Tom Glavine's overpowering performance made him an obvious choice for the Series Most Valuable Player Award.

BRAVO!

on us. … If he wants some, tell him to come over and get some."

Justice finally walked away, saying, "I got to cool down, guys."

The next morning, the headline on the front of the Journal Constitution sports section read: "Justice takes a rip at Braves fans." During batting practice, Justice was surrounded by reporters. He didn't retract his comments, though he would later admit on "The David Letterman Show" that when he saw the paper he was scared to go to the park.

Glavine, however, was not at all nervous about the biggest start of his career. "A lot of people think this is the perfect game for me to pitch," he said before the game. "It would be great to win it, and for David and Lemke to get some big hits and Wohlers to get the save. Those are the guys who have been here the longest."

The Braves followed that script. Justice accounted for the only run with a long homer; Glavine allowed just one hit in eight innings; Wohlers pitched the ninth for the save.

And when it was over, when Wohlers jumped high into the air to start the celebration, the Braves had won the World Series on pitching. The Indians' .291 average in the regular season was the highest in the last 50 years; they hit 111 points lower in these six games. The Braves' victories had come on a one-hitter, a two-hitter and two six-hitters.

Amid the celebration, Mazzone, champagne bottle in hand, was asked about his pitching staff. He answered like a father who had just witnessed his son's first Little League hit. "I'm just so proud I could start crying right here and now," he said.

The Braves and their fans celebrated into the night, and two days later the players rode on firetrucks in a parade down Peachtree Street. Then, just several hundred yards from where they won the title, they got together under a big tent for the last time this year.

They drank a little, ate a little, and talked of what the future would bring.

"I'll really miss these guys," Smoltz said. "It was a great run."

And as they gathered for the final time, behind them sat the golden trophy, gleaming in the afternoon sun.

FRANK NIEMEIR

Game 6: Ted Turner paraded around the infield with the World Series trophy.

FRANK NIEMEIR

BRAVO!

DAVID TULIS

Game 6: David Justice had the right answer for fans who wondered about his controversial comments, belting a long home run and scoring the only run of the game.

1995 WORLD

Row 1: Bat boys Kevin Banks, Chris Ellis, Chris Van Zant, Paul Bodi. **Row 2:** Bill Acree (director of team travel, equipment manager), Rafael Belliard, Ed Giovanolo, Jim Guadagno (coach), Leo Mazzone (coach), Ned Yost (coach), Clarence Jones (coach), Bobby Cox (manager), Jim Beauchamp (coach), Pat Corrales (coach), Jimy Williams (coach), Frank Fultz (coach), Luis Polonia, Mike Mordecai. **Row 3:** Casey Stevenson (clubhouse manager), Mike Devereaux, Jeff

CHAMPIONS

Blauser, Dwight Smith, Brad Clontz, Brad Woodall, Darrell May, Pedro Borbon, Kent Mercker, Eddie Perez, Tom Glavine, Greg Maddux, Marquis Grissom, Dave Pursley (head trainer), Jeff Porter (assistant trainer). Row 4: Terrell Wade, Chipper Jones, Ryan Klesko, Greg McMichael, David Justice, Mark Lemke, Fred McGriff, Tom Thobe, Jason Schmidt, Mark Wohlers, Mike Kelly, John Smoltz, Javier Lopez, Charlie O'Brien, Alejandro Peña, Steve Avery.

Next page: KEVIN KEISTER

YEAR IN REVIEW

No.	Date	Opponent	Score	Winner	Loser	W-L	Pos.	GB
1	4/26	San Francisco	W 12-5	Maddux	Mulholland	1-0	T1	-
2	4/27	San Francisco	W 6-4	Stanton	Burba	2-0	T1	-
3	4/28	at Los Angeles	L 9-1	Daal	Avery	2-1	T1	-
4	4/29	at Los Angeles	W 4-3	McMichael	Murphy	3-1	1	1.0
5	4/30	at Los Angeles	W 6-3	Smoltz	Martinez	4-1	1	1.0
6	5/2	at Florida	W 7-1	Maddux	Gardner	5-1	1	1.0
7	5/3	at Florida	W 6-4	Glavine	Witt	6-1	1	1.0
8	5/4	at Florida	Suspended game, resumed 9/7			6-1	1	1.5
9	5/5	Philadelphia	L 9-4	Green	Merker	6-2	1	1.0
10	5/6	Philadelphia	L 3-1	Mimbs	Smoltz	6-3	T1	-
11	5/7	Philadelphia	L 5-4	Schilling	Bedrosian	6-4	2	1.0
12	5/8	Philadelphia	L 3-2	Abbott	Glavine	6-5	3	2.0
13	5/9	at New York	W 3-2	McMichael	Manzanillo	7-5	2	2.0
14	5/10	at New York	L 5-2	Henry	Wohlers	7-6	2	3.0
15	5/11	at New York	L 5-3	Jones	Smoltz	7-7	3	3.0
16	5/12	Cincinnati	L 5-4	Brantley	Bedrosian	7-8	3	4.0
17	5/13	Cincinnati	W 9-6	Glavine	Smith	8-8	3	4.0
18	5/14	Cincinnati	L 5-3	Carrasco	Clontz	8-9	3	5.0
19	5/15	Colorado	W 4-0	Mercker	Olivares	9-9	3	4.0
20	5/16	Colorado	W 15-3	Smoltz	Acevedo	10-9	3	4.0
21	5/17	Colorado	L 6-5	Holmes	Maddux	10-10	3	5.0
22	5/18	Colorado	W 3-2	McMichael	Munoz	11-10	3	4.5
23	5/19	Florida	W 4-0	Avery	Veres	12-10	T2	3.5
24	5/20	Florida	W 8-7	Wohlers	Nen	13-10	2	3.5
25	5/21	Florida	W 5-1	Smoltz	Burkett	14-10	T1	3.5
26	5/23	at St Louis	W 7-1	Maddux	Jackson	15-10	2	3.5
27	5/24	at St Louis	W 9-5	Glavine	Fascatore	16-10	2	3.5
28	5/25	at St. Louis	L 4-1	Hill	Avery	16-11	2	3.5
29	5/26	at Houston	W 8-3	Mercker	Swindell	17-11	2	3.5
30	5/27	at Houston	L 3-2	Hudek	Stanton	17-12	2	4.5
31	5/28	at Houston	W 3-1	Maddux	Kile	18-12	2	3.5
32	5/29	at Chicago	W 2-1	Glavine	Castillo	19-12	2	3.5
33	5/31	at Chicago	L 4-1	Morgan	Avery	19-13	2	4.0
34	6/1	Los Angeles	L 6-3	Valdes	Mercker	19-14	T2	5.0
35	6/2	Houston	L 7-2	Drabek	Smoltz	19-15	3	5.0
36	6/3	Houston	L 2-1	Jones	Wohlers	19-16	3	5.0
37	6/4	Houston	L 6-2	Reynolds	Glavine	19-17	3	5.0
38	6/5	Chicago	W 7-5	Bedrosian	Hickerson	20-17	3	4.0
39	6/6	Chicago	W 17-3	Mercker	Trachsel	21-17	T2	3.0
40	6/7	Chicago	W 4-3	Smoltz	Perez	22-17	2	3.0
41	6/9	St. Louis	W 3-2	McMichael	Arocha	23-17	2	3.0
42	6/10	St. Louis	L 7-3	Delucia	Glavine	23-18	T2	4.0
43	6/11	St. Louis	L 8-4	Habyan	Avery	23-19	3	5.0
44	6/13	at Montreal	L 11-2	Perez	Mercker	23-20	3	5.0
45	6/14	at Montreal	W 7-3	Smoltx	Fassero	24-20	3	4.0
46	6/15	at Montreal	W 2-0	Maddux	Martinez	25-20	T2	4.0

No.	Date	Opponent	Score	Winner	Loser	W-L	Pos.	GB
47	6/16	at Colorado	W 2-0	Glavine	Swift	26-20	T2	3.0
48	6/17	at Colorado	W 7-1	Avery	Acevedo	27-20	2	3.0
49	6/18	at Colorado	W 9-4	Mercker	Freeman	28-20	2	3.0
50	6/19	at Cincinnati	W 10-0	Smoltz	Schourek	29-20	2	3.0
51	6/20	at Cincinnati	W 10-2	Maddux	Nitkowski	30-20	2	3.0
52	6/21	at Cincinnati	L 3-1	Smiley	Glavine	30-21	2	4.0
53	6/22	at Cincinnati	L 9-8	Hernandez	Borbon	30-22	2	5.0
54	6/23	New York	L 9-3	Saberhagen	Mercker	30-23	2	5.0
55	6/24	New York	W 5-1	Smoltz	Mlicki	31-23	2	5.0
56	6/25	New York	W 4-2	Maddux	Harnisch	32-23	2	5.0
57	6/26	Montreal	W 4-3	Glavine	Aquino	33-23	2	4.5
58	6/27	Montreal	L 3-0	Henry	Avery	33-24	2	4.5
59	6/28	Montreal	W 4-3	Clontz	Rojas	34-24	2	3.5
60	6/30	at Philadelphia	L 3-1	Green	Smoltz	34-25	2	4.0
61	7/1	at Philadelphia	W 3-1	Maddux	West	35-25	2	3.0
62	7/2	at Philadelphia	W 5-3	Glavine	Mimbs	36-25	2	2.0
63	7/3	at Philadelphia	W 10-4	Avery	Schilling	37-25	2	1.0
64	7/4	Los Angeles	W 3-2	Clontz	Valdes	38-25	T1	-
65	7/5	Los Angeles	W 4-1	Wohlers	Astacio	39-25	1	1.0
66	7/6	Los Angeles	W 1-0	McMichael	Seanez	40-25	1	1.0
67	7/7	San Francisco	W 8-4	Glavine	Greer	41-25	1	2.0
68	7/8	San Francisco	W 9-4	Avery	Portugal	42-25	1	3.0
69	7/9	San Francisco	W 3-2	Wohlers	Beck	43-25	1	4.0
70	7/12	at Pittsburgh	L 2-1	Parris	Smoltz	43-26	1	4.0
71	7/13	at San Diego	W 4-1	Maddux	Hamilton	44-26	1	4.0
72	7/14	at San Diego	W 6-2	Glavine	Benes	45-26	1	5.0
73	7/15	at San Diego	W 7-6	Clontz	Florie	46-26	1	6.0
74	7/16	at San Diego	L 3-1	Dishman	Mercker	46-27	1	6.0
75	7/18	Pittsburgh	L 5-4	Dyer	Wohlers	46-28	1	5.5
76	7/19	Pittsburgh	W 3-2	Maddux	Loaiza	47-28	1	6.5
77	7/20	Pittsburgh	W 4-3	Clontz	Plesac	48-28	1	7.5
78	7/21	San Diego	L 9-6	Bochtler	McMichael	48-28	1	6.5
79	7/22	San Diego	W 3-2	Wohlers	Blair	49-29	1	7.5
80	7/23	San Diego	W 2-1	Smoltz	Hamilton	50-29	1	7.5
81	7/24	at Pittsburgh	W 3-2	Clontz	Plesac	51-29	1	8.5
82	7/25	at Pittsburgh	W 3-1	Clontz	Gott	52-29	1	8.5
83	7/26	at Los Angeles	L 1-0	Valdes	Avery	52-30	1	7.0
84	7/27	at Los Angeles	L 9-4	Cummings	Mercker	52-31	1	6.0
85	7/28	at San Francisco	W 6-2	Clontz	Beck	53-31	1	7.0
86	7/29	at San Francisco	W 5-1	Maddux	Mulholland	54-31	1	8.0
87	7/30	at San Francisco	L 3-2	Brewington	Glavine	54-32	1	8.0
88	8/1	Philadelphia	L 4-3	Fernandez	Avery	54-33	1	7.0
89	8/2	Philadelphia	W 7-5	Mercker	Munoz	55-33	1	8.0
90	8/3	Philadelphia	W 5-4	Borbon	Slocumb	56-33	1	9.0
91	8/4	at Montreal	W 4-3	Maddux	Martinez	57-33	1	10.0
92	8/5	at Montreal	W 9-6	Glavine	Henry	58-33	1	11.0
93	8/6	at Montreal	L 6-2	Perez	Avery	58-34	1	11.0
94	8/7	at Montreal	W 5-1	Mercker	Fassero	59-34	1	11.5
95	8/8	Cincinnati	W 5-4	Smoltz	McElroy	60-34	1	12.5
96	8/9	Cincinnati	L 9-3	Burba	Maddux	60-35	1	12.5
97	8/10	Cincinnati	W 2-1	Wohlers	Carrasco	61-35	1	13.5
98	8/11	Colorado	W 5-3	Avery	Reynoso	62-35	1	13.5
99	8/12	Colorado	L 16-4	Leskanic	Mercker	62-36	1	13.5
100	8/13	Colorado	W 3-2	Wohlers	Holmes	63-36	1	14.5
101	8/14	Florida	W 4-3	McMichael	Perez	64-36	1	14.5
102	8/15	Florida	W 4-1	Glavine	Banks	65-36	1	14.5
103	8/16	Florida	L 8-5	Rapp	Avery	65-36	1	14.5
104	8/18	at St. Louis	L 4-3	Watson	Mercker	65-38	1	14.0

No.	Date	Opponent	Score	Winner	Loser	W-L	Pos.	GB
105	8/19	at St. Louis	L 5-4	Urbani	Murray	65-39	1	13.0
106	8/20	at St. Louis	W 1-0	Maddux	Morgan	66-39	1	13.0
107	8/21	at Houston	W 5-4	Glavine	McMurtry	67-39	1	13.0
108	8/22	at Houston	W 6-4	Avery	Brocail	68-39	1	14.0
109	8/23	at Houston	W 6-2	Mercker	Hampton	69-39	1	14.0
110	8/25	at Chicago	W 7-3	Smoltz	Castillo	70-39	1	13.5
111	8/26	at Chicago	W 7-2	Maddux	Trachsel	71-39	1	13.5
112	8/26	at Chicago	W 3-1	Glavine	Bullinger	72-39	1	14.5
113	8/28	at Chicago	L 7-5	Navarro	Avery	72-40	1	14.0
114	8/29	Houston	L 11-9	Swindell	Murray	72-41	1	14.0
115	8/30	Houston	L 2-0	Reynolds	Smoltz	72-42	1	14.0
116	8/31	Houston	W 5-2	Maddux	Drabek	73-42	1	14.0
117	9/1	Chicago	L 7-5	Bullinger	Glavine	73-43	1	14.0
118	9/2	Chicago	L 6-4	Navarro	Avery	73-44	1	14.0
119	9/3	Chicago	W 2-0	Schmidt	Foster	74-44	1	14.0
120	9/4	St. Louis	W 6-5	Wohlers	Parrett	75-44	1	15.0
121	9/5	St. Louis	W 1-0	Maddux	Urbani	76-44	1	16.0
122	9/6	St. Louis	W 6-1	Glavine	Petkovsek	77-44	1	16-0
	9/7	at Florida	W 6-3	Woodall	Nen	78-44	1	16.5
123	9/7	at Florida	L 5-1	Rapp	Avery	78-45	1	15.0
124	9/8	at Florida	W 6-5	McMichael	Perez	79-45	1	17.0
125	9/9	at Florida	W 9-5	Clontz	Nen	80-45	1	17.0
126	9/10	at Florida	L 5-4	Mathews	Borbon	80-46	1	17.0
127	9/11	at Colorado	L 5-4	Hickerson	Woodall	80-47	1	16.5
128	9/12	at Colorado	L 12-2	Painter	Avery	80-48	1	15.5
129	9/13	at Colorado	W 9-7	Schmidt	Bailey	81-48	1	16.5
130	9/15	at Cincinnati	W 3-1	Smoltz	McElroy	82-48	1	17.0
131	9/16	at Cincinnati	W 6-1	Maddux	Portugal	83-48	1	18.0
132	9/17	at Cincinnati	W 4-1	Glavine	Smiley	84-48	1	19.0
133	9/18	New York	W 7-1	Avery	Jones	85-48	1	19.0
134	9/19	New York	L 10-3	Mlickli	Schmidt	85-49	1	19.0
135	9/20	New York	L 8-4	Isringhausen	Smoltz	85-50	1	19.0
136	9/21	New York	W 3-0	Maddux	Telgheder	86-50	1	19.0
137	9/22	Montreal	W 5-1	Glavine	Perez	87-50	1	20.0
138	9/23	Montreal	L 5-2	Martinez	McMichael	87-51	1	19.0
139	9/24	Montreal	W 5-4	Borbon	Leiper	88-51	1	20.0
140	9/26	at Philadelphia	W 5-1	Smoltz	Quantrill	89-51	1	21.0
141	9/27	at Philadelphia	W 6-0	Maddux	Mimbs	90-51	1	22.0
142	9/29	at New York	L 6-3	Jones	Glavine	90-52	1	22.0
143	9/30	at New York	L 8-4	Minor	Schmidt	90-53	1	21.0
144	10/1	at New York	L 1-0	Walker	Wade	90-54	1	21.0

Divisional Playoffs vs. Rockies

No.	Date	Opponent	Score	Winner	Loser	W-L
1	10/3	at Colorado	W 5-4	Peña	Leskanic	1-0
2	10/4	at Colorado	W 7-4	Peña	Munoz	2-0
3	10/6	at Atlanta	L 7-5	Holmes	Wohlers	2-1
4	10/7	at Atlanta	W 10-4	Maddux	Saberhagen	3-1

League Championship vs. Reds

No.	Date	Opponent	Score	Winner	Loser	W-L
1	10/10	at Cincinnati	W 2-1	Wohlers	Jackson	1-0
2	10/11	at Cincinnati	W 6-2	McMichael	Portugal	2-0
3	10/13	Atlanta	W 5-2	Maddux	Wells	3-0
4	10/14	Atlanta	W 6-0	Avery	Schourek	4-0

World Series vs. Indians

No.	Date	Opponent	Score	Winner	Loser	W-L
1	10/21	Atlanta	W 3-2	Maddux	Hershiser	1-0
2	10/22	Atlanta	W 4-3	Glavine	Martinez	2-0
3	10/24	at Cleveland	L 7-6	Mesa	Pena	2-1
4	10/25	at Cleveland	W 3-1	Avery	Hill	3-1
5	10/26	at Cleveland	L 5-4	Hershiser	Maddux	3-2
6	10/28	Atlanta	W 1-0	Glavine	Martinez	4-2

THE 1995 ATLANTA BRAVES

RICH ADDICKS